PRAISE FOR
GOOD IDEAS FOR GOOD TEACHERS WHO WANT GOOD JOBS

Full of common-sense advice for the ambitious teacher, at any stage of their career, who wishes to take control of their career path. It is certainly a must-read for those wishing to make healthy career choices. The section on paying attention to your public profile is particularly relevant at the moment. Certainly one I will be recommending to staff at my school. The key points summaries at the end of each chapter are useful little 'notelets'. The illustrations are perfect, and made me smile, and the thought-provoking questions throughout the text are cleverly written and make you think more carefully about the decisions you make.

Beverley Dandy, Head Teacher, Outwoods Primary School

Imagine the scene. You meet an old and trusted friend in a coffee shop for a catch-up and, as naturally happens, the subject of work comes up. You admit to thinking about moving on but aren't sure. At this point your old and trusted friend begins to expertly help you unpick and explore your thoughts about a new job. After a long, caffeine-fuelled, discussion you have your eureka moment and your future career is paved in yellow bricks ahead of you. Easy. But for those of us without such a friend, where do we go to get our thinking unpicked? Grab a coffee and get ready to decide whether you're a 'gunner' or a 'doer'!

Gerald Haigh provides a fully comprehensive toolkit of thoughts, prompts, key ideas and questions to help us consider our current role and potential new roles. Every aspect of the procedure is considered from motivation to move (or stay put), applications, school visits, the interview process and, finally, dealing with the outcome. As a head teacher who has interviewed a decent number (and range) of candidates, this book still gave me tips, tricks and food for thought. One important point to note here is that Gerald never preaches. In fact the book is written in a challenging but supportive way and he maintains a 'coaching' feel throughout. His use of humour is great (I love his analogy involving a hearing-aid beige used car) making a relatively serious subject light-hearted and entertaining. I must admit I expected a book about getting a job to be fairly dull, but the writing style and organisation of the information into easily readable chunks meant I read far more than I expected to in one sitting. My only concern is that, with an increased number of good candidates to choose from, this book may make the recruitment process even harder – what a great problem to have!

Just about everyone needs to read this book. Even if you are part of the foundations of your school, and have no intention of moving on, this book will help you evaluate your decisions and aspirations. Oh, and despite the title, I'm sure even the outstanding teachers are allowed to read it!

Paul Bannister, Head Teacher, Jerudong International School

All the things that your supportive boss hoped that you would osmotically pick up! Good teachers will be great if they take these tips on board.

Sir Mark Grundy, Shireland Collegiate Academy

Gerald Haigh is one of the most insightful and experienced education writers. His wisdom has graced the pages of SecEd for several years and the publication is all the stronger for it.

Pete Henshaw, Editor, SecEd Magazine

GOOD IDEAS
FOR GOOD TEACHERS
WHO WANT GOOD JOBS

GERALD HAIGH

Crown House Publishing Limited
www.crownhouse.co.uk

Revised and updated edition first published by

Crown House Publishing
Crown Buildings, Bancyfelin, Carmarthen, Wales, SA33 5ND, UK
www.crownhouse.co.uk

and

Crown House Publishing Company LLC
6 Trowbridge Drive, Suite 5, Bethel, CT 06801-2858, USA
www.crownhousepublishing.com

First published 2015.

First published as *Jobs and Interviews Pocketbook* (ISBN: 978-190377678-0)

British Library of Cataloguing-in-Publication Data

A catalogue entry for this book is available from the British Library.

Print ISBN 978-184590951-2
Mobi ISBN 978-184590967-3
ePub ISBN 978-184590968-0
ePDF ISBN 978-184590969-7

LCCN 2015909512

Printed and bound in the UK by

Bell & Bain Ltd., Thornliebank, Glasgow

To all new and aspiring teachers, embarking on what is surely the best and most worthwhile job of all.

CONTENTS

INTRODUCTION

You're a good teacher. Don't be modest: you know you are. All the signs are there – your students make progress and behave themselves, colleagues trust and respect you, performance reviews are positive, parents are friendly at open evenings, the head teacher laughs and nods at your staff party karaoke performances, the caretaker did you a favour and got you a cheap car battery, and as for the inspectors … OK, we won't go there.

Now, because you're good, you believe it's time you moved to a position that's better for you than the one you're currently in.

Of course you do. What would be the point of moving to something worse? How foolish would that be? Not, as we shall see, foolish enough to prevent lots of people doing it – which is one reason why you should read this book.

But I'm not here just to stop you from making mistakes – although that comes into it. My real aim is to make sure that, as you approach each step on the career ladder, the choices you make and the actions you take are really worthy of your status as a good teacher. That's to say, they are deeply considered, well researched, honest, self-aware and carried out with confidence and professionalism. Or, to put it a bit more simply, I want you to be able to say, after you've applied and been interviewed, as you wait for the decision: 'That definitely is the right job for me. I want it, and I know I've given it my best shot.'

GOOD TEACHERS ARE FLEXIBLE VISIONARIES

GOOD TEACHERS ARE FLEXIBLE VISIONARIES

What does that mean? Quite simply, good teachers have an eye for where they might be going, and yet are alert and ready to dodge across to another path.

MOBILITY

Very few long-serving teachers are working in the school in which they started. As time's gone on, they've taken advantage of the fact that the great thing about teaching is that it happens everywhere. Find a community of human beings, look around and there'll be at least one teacher.

A friend of mine, a good teacher, decided to do two years with VSO (Voluntary Service Overseas). She was sent to a remote community in the high Himalayas, where she taught wonderful children who were eager to learn.

My friend could do that because she was a good teacher. (VSO has a rigorous and lengthy selection process.) Now, as a result, she's an even better teacher, back in her home town as a class teacher in a challenging school.

That's the kind of choice you have. As a good teacher, you can carve out the career that suits you – on a ladder leading to headship and beyond, or on a winding and intriguing path through a series of jobs that broaden your experience of life.

CAREER PLAN

Does that mean you need a career plan?

That's not an easy question to answer. Here's what two long-serving teachers think.

I knew straight away what I wanted to do. I was going to be in my first headship by 35, do five years in it then move to a much bigger school, drive its results up and end up with an OBE or better. I worked hard, got promotion at every opportunity, following the jobs wherever they led, and it has all worked really well for me. I retired at 52 and now do quite a lot of lucrative consultancy.

Plan? No fear. I did teacher training to be near my partner, took a job at my placement school and stayed there for two years. Then my partner left me, so I went to China for a while and did some English teaching. When I got back I did supply teaching in some difficult schools. I seemed able to cope, and was offered a permanent job in a unit for kids with behavioural problems. There was a lot of staff movement; I ended up running it, and that's what I still do. It's been a roller coaster and I wouldn't have missed any of it.

Which is correct, then? Make a plan, or go with the flow?

Obviously, it depends on what sort of person you are. That said, most of us have one eye on the immediate future. Maybe you've had at least one of these thoughts:

You look at your head teacher and think, 'That'll be me before too long.'

You look at your head teacher and think, 'No thanks. My future's with kids. I want to stay in the classroom.'

You look at your bank balance and think, 'I wonder if I could get by on four days a week?'

You look at a country, or a group of children with particular needs, and think, 'Those kids need me.'

If you have even tentatively pondered any of these (there are others; these are just examples) then you already have some kind of embryo career plan – call it 'Career Plan

Stage 1'. Recognise it, talk about it, think it through. Then at some point you might think it is worth moving to Stage 2.

Stage 2 simply means pinning down what your next step is going to be. So if your aim is a headship, it's about what you can do right now to help that come about. Start becoming professionally qualified? Look for a step up the ladder? Seek more responsibility in your present job?

And if your aim is to stay in the classroom, what steps can you take to become recognised as an excellent practitioner, a mentor to others and a leader of learning?

But don't fill in too much detail, because things may change. Experience, relationships, health, absorbing outside interests can all play havoc with plans that are too closely written. So, be prepared to follow the road, to seize the day.

But whatever unfolds, never look back and wallow in regret.

KEY POINTS

- Have a career plan, but keep it flexible, and always be prepared to rip it up and write a new one.
- Whether you have a long-term strategy or not, always have an eye on your next step.
- If you think you see an opportunity, never be afraid to ask about it.

GOOD TEACHERS MOVE TO GOOD JOBS FOR GOOD REASONS

GOOD TEACHERS MOVE TO GOOD JOBS FOR GOOD REASONS

Because teaching has for so long been a mobile profession, you may well have an inbuilt assumption that you will eventually move on from where you are.

That being so, you need add to that assumption one that says, whenever you do move, at whatever career stage from newly qualified to executive principal, it will be for a positive reason, and to a job you really want.

Well, excuse me? You wouldn't move to a job you didn't want, would you?

Of course not. It's just that many people do. They take a new job, whether first job, or a promotion, and work through the inevitable early feelings of dislocation and unfamiliarity only to find the initial discomfort isn't going away. Gradually, despite strong efforts at denial to self, family, cat and canary, it becomes apparent that they're in the wrong job. All that remains is to make the best of things while waiting for the first decent opportunity to leave. (And as an aside, let's just point out that looking for the first available exit is a sure-fire way of replaying the 'frying pan and fire' metaphor in living colour.)

But you're a good teacher. All the evidence speaks to the truth of that, which makes it really important that you have confidence in yourself and avoid being side-tracked into unsuitable career moves. So, for starters, here are three 'keep the faith' reminders:

- **It's your own career you're interested in.**

  Just because people you know, trained with or worked alongside are 'getting on' does not mean they are making better decisions. The reverse may well be the case.

- **Be prepared to wait**.

  Do your job, build up goodwill, add to your CV, demonstrate your strengths, keep reading job ads, going to teacher gatherings, and keeping your eyes and ears open, and sooner or later the opportunity will come. It's like the search for a good used car. You want the two-litre 'R' model in opalescent red, with leather upholstery and sports suspension, so wait for it and don't be pushed into the 'S' version in hearing-aid beige that happens to be in stock.

- **Rise above current discomfort**.

  The fact that you don't like your current job should make you more, rather than less, discerning about where you want to work in future.

YOUR PRIORITIES

What are you looking for in a new job? Status, money and security come into it, but it's foolish to assume that they are overwhelmingly important to the kind of people who become teachers. There's much more to teaching than that.

Let's do a 'keep your feet on the ground' exercise and list what you expect to find in a new job. List all the necessary features, the absence of any of which will give you pause. Here's my list. Use it as the basis for your own – drop the ones you dislike, and add any you prefer.

YOUR IDEAL JOB

- The more you learn about the job, the more you want to get started.
- It will be in a school that's efficient and orderly both in classrooms and around the buildings.
- It will offer you the chance to develop your own vision of education.
- Your colleagues will be visibly at ease with each other and with their work, ready to support keen newcomers.
- Your students will be open, smiling, well behaved but not cowed, funny but not insolent.
- You will work ethically and honestly in an open and supportive environment.

- Your responsibilities will be clearly defined to you and your colleagues.

- You will work within a planned programme of professional development run by a responsible member of staff.

- You must have the opportunity to use to the full your ever-growing experience, specialist knowledge and skills.

- The post will offer a clearly visible way forward to something better – that is, it's not an obvious dead end.

There are others, but these are the basics. It won't have escaped your notice that they're very much linked – if one's there, it's likely that the others will be too. Think about it, and you'll see that where a number of these factors are missing, and bearing in mind that some are more fundamental than others, it's likely that at the very least it will be difficult to extract professional satisfaction from your role.

SEEKING A CHALLENGE

There are some gifted and driven teachers, of course, who will deliberately move, often as senior leaders, to schools that are dysfunctional and demoralised. They're often motivated – and I've heard it put in these exact words – by the conviction that 'These kids need me.' All I can say is, if you think you're that kind of person, be ruthlessly frank with yourself about your capabilities and experience, and also ask lots of people whose opinion you trust whether they truly believe you can do it. Perhaps you can. There are those that do – I could easily name several. But, as with all parachuted-in heroes, some are captured and shot before they have a chance to display their qualities.

KEY POINTS

- Always have one eye (and ear) on the job market.
- Have ideas about your next job, but keep them flexible.
- Know your capabilities.
- Discuss career ideas and plans with trusted colleagues.

GOOD TEACHERS PAY ATTENTION TO THEIR PUBLIC PROFILE

GOOD TEACHERS PAY ATTENTION TO THEIR PUBLIC PROFILE

From the very start of your teaching career – and probably before – it is a good idea to pay attention to how you are judged as a professional person with responsibility for the safety and welfare of other people's children. The 'spare time' activities of teachers have always been likely to be noticed and judged more stringently than those of, say, investment bankers. Now, though, the internet, and particularly social media, opens up our lives to the whole world, for good or ill.

So, for example, if you express interest in a teaching job, whether it's your first or the last one before retirement, will your prospective employers trawl your social media activity to see what you get up to?

It's certainly routine practice for recruiters in other parts of the working world. The UK recruitment blog the Undercover Recruiter[1] reported on a survey showing that 91 per cent of a sample of 300 employers use social media to screen candidates. Of these, 69 per cent have turned down applicants because of what they found. On the other hand, 68 per cent have actually hired people on the strength of a social media check.

---

1   See: http://theundercoverrecruiter.com/.

SOCIAL MEDIA ACTIVITY

Evidence of employers checking the social media activity of prospective candidates in education is thin, and it seems likely to be less common than the Undercover Recruiter survey reports for other jobs – but it's certain to increase.

One head asked about this said:

We do not check as a matter of course but will use social media if we are struggling to shortlist. On occasion we have enormous fields and at this point it becomes helpful – someone playing piano or engaging in sport is more likely to be shortlisted than the candidate downing a pint of beer (obvious, and yet I've seen it time and time again).

Among actual examples provided by head teachers is one of a candidate for a senior post discovered to be routinely criticising his current head – in obscene terms – to 'friends'.

Given the number of teachers who find themselves in trouble for social media carelessness, the case for routine checking is probably strong. In 2013, Victoria Briggs was reported in the New Teachers section of the *TES* discussing a huge increase in calls from teachers needing guidance:

> While there are instances of pupils setting up fake social media accounts in a teacher's name, the majority of problems are the result of teaching staff themselves behaving inappropriately. More often than not, it's a failure of basic common sense on the part of professionals.[2]

Individual cases mentioned by teaching unions and other organisations tend to be about sheer silliness ('stupidity' might be a better word) rather than anything really sinister. Boasting about 'partying' and drinking, for example, is relatively common among young people, but teachers who have been too open on social media about this aspect of their lives have been taken aback to find themselves in trouble. The self-defeating phrase 'don't tell anyone' even appears in some questionable posts.

It's always been easy for teachers to make mistakes – to be seen falling into the bushes outside the pub, or behaving embarrassingly at an upmarket dinner attended by governors. Up until very recently, though, the effects were local. If you went for an interview in Sheffield, the governors didn't know you'd been thrown out of a club in Basingstoke the night before.

Now, though, the concept of a private life separate from a professional one has been eroded to the point where it hardly exists.

---

2   Victoria Briggs. 'Be smart when it comes to using social media', *New Teachers* (February 2013). Available at: http://newteachers.tes.co.uk/content/be-smart-when-it-comes-using-social-media.

WHAT SHOULD YOU DO?

Starting right now – don't wait until you're a job seeker – pay attention to your social media presence. In short, clean it up. Remember these points:

- Never use bad language. Never criticise your school, your colleagues, your students – and the same goes for other schools you're connected with.

- Check back for bad-tempered or ill-thought-out posts and photographs in the past and remove them.

- Students are interested in you. Innocent photographs – you on a beach, or in fancy dress, or relaxing with friends – can seem less innocent when circulated among teenagers.

- Remember any photograph of you taken by someone else can end up being available to the world.

- If you see a dodgy photograph of yourself on somebody else's site, do your best to get it taken down. Keep the evidence of how well you've tried.

- Check your name on search engines. Stuff you may have forgotten about often seems to have been given the gift of eternal life.

- Never 'friend' a student, of whatever age, on a social media site.

- Be security conscious – use strong passwords, keep your privacy settings tight – for example, ensure non-friends can't see your posts on Facebook – and remember to log out.

- Do as you would be done by – treat others as well as you want to be treated, look after colleagues and draw their attention to anything you think they need to know about.

- Study published advice such as Childnet's Social Networking Guide for Teachers.[3]

- Have a simple and professional email address. If you adopted a jokey, racy one as a student, now's the time to change it. (That's good advice for your students, too, as they approach the end of their schooling.)

BUT IT'S NOT ALL BAD NEWS

My advice is not to keep away from social media completely. Many teachers across the world have developed a respected online presence, for example through thoughtful blogs, relevant Twitter comments and discussion. Twitter, particularly, is regarded by many teachers as a valuable way to exchange professional

---

3   See: http://www.childnet.com/resources/
    social-networking-a-guide-for-teachers-and-professionals.

knowledge. In a few cases this has led to speaking engagements, and occasionally to being consulted by government. And beyond the world of education, evidence of constructive spare time activities – music, fund raising, sport, community groups – can also have a positive effect.

KEY POINTS

- As a teacher, be prepared to accept restrictions on what counts as your private life.

- Try to be aware of how you might look in an informal photograph.

- Do not express extreme religious or political opinions online.

- If you have a rich and positive online presence, present it well.

GOOD TEACHERS KNOW WHEN IT'S TIME TO MOVE ON

GOOD TEACHERS KNOW WHEN IT'S TIME TO MOVE ON

THAT RESTLESS FEELING

You'll hear many teachers say, either directly to friends and colleagues or perhaps as a muttered aside in a fraught staff meeting, 'I'm beginning to think it's time I moved on.'

What, exactly, provokes that thought?

For some, it's just a feeling in the bones, the cumulative effect of many factors, some quite inconsequential taken on their own. Here's what one teacher, in her late thirties, had to say:

I was on the senior leadership team, I'd just got my NPQH (National Professional Qualification for Headship). The head was leaving, a very different sort of person had been appointed from outside and the deputy was going to stay on. I gave a much praised speech at the head's retirement do, feeling confident on the stage before all the invited guests. When I walked back to my table, with applause and nods and smiles all around, I suddenly realised I'd outgrown the role I was in and I knew I had to start the very next day looking at deputy headships.

Others, quite reasonably, want rather more solid reasons than that. For example:

- You are qualified, experienced and feel both competent and impatient for more responsibility.

- There's no obvious opening coming in your present school.

- Even if there is, you aren't convinced that you want to work with the current team.

- Your family life offers a window of opportunity – children about to change schools, you want a house move, your partner's about to change jobs.

Each of those, of course, begs a host of follow-up questions. How, for example, do you know you are qualified and experienced to do a higher level job? Do you have anything to prove it? Better still, have you filled in temporarily at a more senior level? You need hard evidence that you can write down on application forms, and talk about in interviews.

Likewise, don't take it for granted that there are no in-house openings. Future possibilities should always be a theme in performance reviews – if your reviewer doesn't bring the subject up, then you should raise it yourself. It's unlikely any senior leader will make promises to you about promotion, but often you can pick up a good sense of whether and how you might be involved in future developments.

And as to changes in personal or family life, all that's very much an individual matter – except that it's important to take the long-term view. How often is your partner moved around for work? How long will your children be in school? What seems right today may not look so good in three years' time.

To summarise: when you get that moving feeling, take care to give it substance, beginning to build the evidence that will justify whatever you decide to do.

THE LOYALTY FACTOR

It's not all about you. A decision to leave throws up questions of your responsibility to the school, the staff and the students. You must judge all of that for yourself, but the important thing is not to ignore it. Some of the relevant factors include:

- The professional development investment that the school has made in you – particularly, perhaps, if you arrived newly qualified.

- Projects you have initiated and always planned to see through.

- Students who are very dependent on you – with special needs or with exams coming up, for example.

All of that can make life emotionally difficult, and you will want to talk things out with your family and with trusted friends and colleagues. But in the end, it's a decision that all dedicated teachers face. It goes with the job, and only you can tackle it.

CAN'T STAND YOUR CURRENT JOB ANY LONGER?

It would be foolish to ignore the fact that many who leave their jobs do so because of sheer unhappiness and frustration. It's easy for the outside adviser to say, 'Maybe if you do this, or that, you can make things better', but, frankly, in many cases, leaving as soon as possible is the only remaining thing to do. In that case: look forward. Whatever your reasons for wanting to leave, don't dwell on them.

Even if you are consumed by deep and bitter frustration and unhappiness, it's crucial that you deliberately set out to leave those feelings behind. You must see your move entirely in terms of the opportunities and experiences that lie ahead. There are two reasons for this.

First, and most obvious, you need to preserve your mental and emotional health, not only for your sake but for your loved ones. We've all met people who walk around burdened by resentment over past injustices, which they will endlessly pick over and describe to whoever happens to be nearby.

Second, and more immediately practical, is that if you leave, you will be presenting yourself to a prospective employer as a keen, up-for-it candidate whose professional life so far has been a story of enthusiasm and success. You must let nothing – not a casual word, a grimace, an unwise sentence in an application – get in the way of that. As one head commented to me, 'If you're desperate to leave your present job, it's likely to show.'

GUNNERS AND DOERS

Finally, in this section, let's think for a moment about those indecisive souls who think it's time to move on but cannot bring themselves to do anything about it. These are the ones who are 'gunners' as opposed to 'doers':

You watch, I'm gunner apply for
deputy headships this year.

Are you one of those? Here's the test. Is there a role you've always fancied, and bored everyone's pants off about, and is probably within your reach?

In the past twelve months, have you made the slightest attempt to do anything about it?

If you've answered 'yes' then 'no', then, face it, you're a gunner.

Why are you a gunner? Usually it's because you're stuck in your comfort zone. It's too much of an effort to move. But beware. In time, inevitably, the school will change around you. And your comfort zone can so easily disappear.

KEY POINTS

- Observe the progress of others, but learn not to copy them.
- Talk about your job plans, but don't broadcast them.
- Temper ambition with realism.

GOOD TEACHERS KNOW
WHEN TO STAY PUT

GOOD TEACHERS KNOW WHEN TO STAY PUT

Most of this book is about leaving one school to take up a job in another. But ambition takes many forms, and a good teacher may well choose to say: 'If you want to know my career aim, it is to buckle down and do a good job right here, improving the life chances of children in this great local community. Frankly, I like it here and I want to stay.'

Who would criticise that? Or fail to respect their decision and offer advice?

PART OF THE FOUNDATIONS

Almost every school, after all, has someone whose long-term presence and commitment provides stability and continuity, a person who is well known, respected and loved by generations. In 2001 I wrote a *TES* article on long-serving teachers which paid particular tribute to John Lawrence, then retiring after serving the whole of his 43-year career teaching chemistry at Bablake School in Coventry, where he had also been a pupil.[1] He was clear about the path he had chosen, firmly based in the classroom in direct contact with students: 'Teaching doesn't give you much of a financial reward, but it gives

---

1   Gerald Haigh. 'Old School Ties', *TES* (31 August 2001). Available at: http://www.tes.co.uk/teaching-resource/Old-school-ties-350886/.

you emotional satisfaction. Is that the right word? I suppose it is. You feel you've done something for society, and that's what makes this an enjoyable job.'

Would any current go-getter dare to call Mr Lawrence a stick-in-the-mud or, worse, any kind of failure? I sincerely hope not.

(Sadly, John Lawrence died in 2007, while still working part-time at Bablake as the school's archivist. He is commemorated in a memorial garden in the grounds of his beloved school, near the science block.)

Here, though, it's necessary to insert a 'however'. HOWEVER ... just to cloud the idyll a little, I need to point out that, of the seven schools in which I taught, four no longer exist and the remaining three have changed out of all recognition. In each case I was gone by the time the earth tremors really arrived, but some of the colleagues who stayed to the bitter end found themselves facing redundancy or forced redeployment to less happy new pastures. The sober truth is that if you cling on for too long, the world will always change around you, possibly to the point where you may lose control of your job, your future and, possibly, your health and well-being.

So, a good teacher who has made the positive decision to stay put will constantly ask, and discuss with others, these key questions.

- Is my stay-put policy positive, or am I just fearful of change?
- Have I sound reasons for believing my job will be here in five years?
- Is it possible that my school will significantly change, or even close?
- Staying here, will I continue to develop professionally, through continuing professional development (CPD) and/or varied opportunities to contribute to the school?
- If there are internal changes, are there identifiable alternative routes for me within the school?
- If profound structural change appears on the horizon, do I have a viable plan B, kept up to date?
- If, in, say, five years, I am forced to move, how marketable will I be?

Add to that list any factors that are particular to you and your job and then keep it constantly under review. Adopt the old sailor's doctrine, which says, 'Keep one hand for yourself and one for the ship.'

KEY POINTS

- Staying put must be for positive, not fearful, reasons.
- Keep looking ahead for any pitfalls.
- Seek to grow in your chosen role.
- Use your experience to support colleagues.

GOOD TEACHERS KNOW HOW THE JOB MARKET WORKS

GOOD TEACHERS KNOW HOW THE JOB MARKET WORKS

You won't get a job unless you study the market, so you need to have some basic understanding of how the whole business works. It can look mysterious and complicated from the outside, and in some ways it is. Cut through the jargon and bureaucracy, though, and you end up with a series of easy-to-follow steps.

A VACANCY IS IDENTIFIED AND DEFINED

That's done by the authority or organisation which runs the school, obviously in close consultation with the school leadership.

It may be a new post, in line with the growth of the school, a replacement for a teacher who's moved on, or a combination of both – a new post that includes the duties of an earlier one. It may be a full- or part-time permanent post, or a temporary appointment defined by a fixed-term contract.

Temporary posts in general, and one-year contracts in particular, are much more common than they once were. This is because for some years now schools have been living through major changes in curriculum and organisation, and have had to be ready to adapt the shape of the teaching force at relatively short notice.

The school's leadership will have a good general idea of what kind of person they're looking for. They may decide they could accept a newly qualified applicant. In fact, sometimes they will positively encourage applications from new teachers. Or they may want specific qualifications and experience, such as a good class of degree, or a share of leadership in a specialist subject, or a background in special needs.

ONE EYE ON THE BUDGET

Cost comes into the decision, of course. Teachers come, to put it crudely, at a range of different prices. The cheapest ones are those straight out of training, who will be given little or no extra formal responsibility over and above their basic teaching. There's a cost involved in training and mentoring a new teacher, but it's still true that the least expensive way to run a school is to staff it largely with newly qualified teachers. It would rarely be a wise policy, but it's true that when a highly paid teacher leaves, governors will often suggest taking the opportunity to make a substantial saving by recruiting someone who can legitimately be paid much less. Also, many schools look for regular injections of an often ill-defined quality described in terms such as youth, new blood, fresh ideas and so on, which a newly qualified teacher may bring.

However, this means that relatively inexperienced or newly qualified job-seekers must not assume that they are automatically at a disadvantage in comparison with experienced candidates. The opposite may well be the case.

THE POST IS ADVERTISED

The people who write teaching job adverts usually know their business well, and can word them to draw the attention of the kind of person they're looking for and fend off those who have no chance. Frequently, conditions – experience, qualifications – are specified in the advertisement with the intention both of attracting suitable candidates and heading off applications that would be weeded out at the first reading. But they know that some ambitious folk will take a stab at a job which seems out of reach, and that it sometimes pays off.

AN APPLICATION PACK IS SENT OUT OR, MORE USUALLY, MADE AVAILABLE ONLINE VIA A LINK ON THE SCHOOL WEBSITE, AND APPLICATIONS AWAITED

Some days after the closing date for applications, representatives of the school choose and notify a number of people to be interviewed. Meanwhile, references will be sought for some of the candidates.

INTERVIEWS ARE HELD

After this, a candidate is offered the job, which he or she will be expected to accept promptly.

There are variations on that basic pattern. Inevitably, there are times when a school's leadership or governors are interested in someone, perhaps an internal candidate, who is then 'invited to apply', and professional head-hunters are often involved in recruiting for difficult-to-fill senior leadership posts.

In the end, though, one of the most reassuring aspects of the schools job market is the persistence, throughout many changes in how schools are run, of the honest principle of open advertisement and competitive application and interview. It's a process that many, perhaps most, teachers will go through several times in their career. Then eventually, as they move into middle and senior leadership, they see the process from both sides.

WHAT THIS MEANS FOR CANDIDATES

Think about this process, and you can see that it is not an area of life where someone in the pub says, 'We've got just the job for you – when can you start?'

People do sometimes hear of teaching jobs by word of mouth in meetings and at conferences and from social media contacts, but even then they have to take part in the standard application process.

In reality, then, seeking and chasing down a job will take up a lot of time. But if you're serious about it, you have to see it through, meticulously, honestly and accurately. Later, we'll look at some of the problems that can be caused by a failure to take care.

KEY POINTS

- Be prepared to spend a lot of time on your job search.

- Be focused, but also be ready to run with the wild card.

- Have faith. Take the advert at face value and apply.

GOOD TEACHERS CHOOSE PROSPECTIVE JOBS WELL

GOOD TEACHERS CHOOSE PROSPECTIVE JOBS WELL

TAKE THE TIME TO CAST YOUR NET WIDELY

You may be sure you know exactly what sort of job you want. That's fine, but you should spend some time browsing areas beyond your immediate focus – different types of school, different areas of responsibility, other regions, other countries even. It's possible you will be attracted by a post you didn't even know existed, at home or abroad.

If you're interested in a particular school, or group of schools, then keep an eye on their websites, because vacancies sometimes emerge there. News that a teacher is leaving, for example, may alert you to watch out for his/ her job being advertised.

Right. You've studied the adverts and identified some jobs that you want to look at. You think there's at least a chance that you've spotted one or more that ticks at least some of your 'ideal job' boxes. First, though, before you take the next step, read the advice in this chapter.

READ EACH ADVERT CAREFULLY

Pick up the detail. It's important, for example, to understand what kind of school it is. There's a wide variety these days – independent schools, faith schools, academies, free schools and studio schools as well as local authority maintained schools. The point here is that not all schools have the same terms and conditions of service, or the same pension arrangements.

Next, what's the salary level? Where exactly is the job? Is it permanent or temporary? Full- or part-time? Is the word 'experienced' in the advert? Are extra qualifications mentioned? The right advert will cause many readers to shake their heads and turn the page, and a few to jump up from their seats in excitement.

For example, this excerpt from a real advert for a primary deputy asks for someone who:

- is a successful classroom practitioner across the primary school age range
- has a clear strategic vision for teaching and learning
- has a passion for generating an energetic and creative learning environment
- has a commitment to working closely with the whole community
- is committed to leading the extended provision in the community.

Some are general qualities which ought to be taken for granted. Two in particular, though, are more specific. Can you see what they are?

'Across the primary school age range' may shut out anyone who's worked exclusively in either a junior or infant school. It might be worth politely asking about that in advance.

The repeated emphasis on 'community' and 'extended provision' says they want someone to develop the school's community links and out of hours provision.

CONSIDER THE PRACTICALITIES

Discuss with family and friends exactly what working arrangements you need, or are prepared to accept. Would you settle for part-time, or temporary, or both, if the job's right in other ways? Bear in mind that it's not only acceptable but often necessary to call and clarify in advance. For example, if a job is advertised as part-time, it can matter very much whether or not you have any choice of when you will be asked to work.

CHECK HOW MUCH NOTICE YOU WILL NEED TO GIVE

Based on what the advert says about when the job starts, how much notice will you have to give to your present school if you're successful? It can vary according to your contract and the time of year. Check with your employer or with your written contract; don't rely on what friends and colleagues say.

GET THE DETAILS

If you like the look of a job, obtain the details that are mentioned above. If the advert is online this is likely to mean just clicking to download the documents. Typically, what comes will be:

- **A description of the school**, emphasising successful aspects, with a photograph of the best bits of the building. If the school has been judged outstanding by Ofsted the details will invariably say so, and particularly good exam results will also be highlighted, often in considerable proud detail.

- **A job description** for the advertised post – statutory responsibilities, precise curriculum areas/exams, details of the department and how the job sits within it. Is the job new, or filling a vacancy? If it's new, is the

leadership looking for an innovator? If the description
does not say, make sure you find out, if and when you
are interviewed.

- **A person specification** – this describes the notional
  person that they see filling the job. It's really important
  to see it as exactly that. This means it isn't just asking
  you for a statement of your astonishing capabilities.
  Your application, if and when you write it, should be
  completed with the person specification at your side
  – or sharing the screen on your computer, so study it
  very carefully. It may well dawn on you either that you
  are totally unfitted for the job and may as well give up
  right now – or the job has been uncannily devised
  with you in mind.

- **An application form** – This asks you to fill in the
  formal gaps – dates and brief details of your career
  up to now, qualifications, key CPD landmarks. Details
  of referees usually go here. Often there's a space for a
  personal statement. If not, there will be a request for a
  separate letter. The form, and the letter, will call for
  painstaking care, as we shall see.

KEEP THINGS ORGANISED

You may well end up with details of several jobs. Don't get them muddled. Keep them carefully, whether as hard copy or online files, and read each of them several times because you will surely find something really important on the second, third or any subsequent check.

In particular, for each of the jobs, make a note of the closing date for applications. Then double-check it, and set up any necessary calendar alerts.

How foolish would you feel if you missed your dream job because you had the wrong application closing date fixed in your mind? It does happen.

ADD TO THE PICTURE

For each job, try to construct as full a picture as possible. Use the application pack details and the school website (which may well be the route to the application pack). Make a note of the number of pupils on roll, any plans for the future, any immediate challenges, and notice anything that the school wishes to highlight as its specialisms or achievements. Here are some examples. Many others are possible.

- A particular subject specialism.
- A special unit – such as for children with sensory impairments.
- A listed building.
- A reputation for drama productions.
- A strong musical tradition.

There may be an opportunity to mention these in your application or at the interview.

You can also look at the school's most recent Ofsted report and exam/test results, all of which are available online – though successful schools often include the links in their details. Only you can decide whether, and how, to be influenced by them, but they are useful to know.

An internet search on the school will usually turn up more information, such as local newspaper articles. However, read them with caution and an open mind.

One head teacher says: 'The application pack doesn't just give you information. It implicitly gives you hints and prompts for you to use in your application and – you hope – in your interview.'

SEEK HELP

Whether you've made many or no applications before, don't be afraid to get help at every stage. So, for example, ask trusted, knowledgeable and experienced friends who know you well to read the job details and give you frank feedback about whether, and how, you should take your application forward. *But* keep your own counsel and be prepared to back your own judgement. Consulting means just that. In the end, the decision is entirely yours.

KEY POINTS

- Read the job details dispassionately and critically.
- Consider the broader effects of you taking the job – on your family, for example.
- Consult with trusted colleagues, but own your decisions.

GOOD TEACHERS DO GOOD GROUNDWORK FOR THEIR APPLICATIONS

GOOD TEACHERS DO GOOD GROUNDWORK FOR THEIR APPLICATIONS

Let's assume you now have one or two jobs for which you are definitely going to apply. You have the details, and you're ready to start on the form. Before that, though, there are still some conventions and rules to be ticked off.

VISIT THE SCHOOL

At this point, before you actually apply, you should visit the school if you possibly can. The way you handle school visits – even the briefest of pop-ins – is really important, and for that reason we'll deal with school visits in a section of its own; see page 67.

CLEAR UP UNCERTAINTIES

Be sure you know exactly what you're applying for. If there's anything you're unsure of, it's OK to phone, write or email for clarification. Or, of course, if you visit, you should have the opportunity to ask the right questions. Sensible requests for further information, clearly and courteously put, whether in person or otherwise, present you as a serious candidate who is genuinely interested in the school and the job.

For example, if you don't quite tick all the boxes in the advert, but still feel very capable of doing the job, try writing or emailing with a question. For example:

'Your advertisement …

'uses the phrase "experienced teacher". Would you accept an application from a mature NQT (newly qualified teacher)?'

'says part-time. Would there be an opportunity to negotiate on the hours?'

'says the job is a one-year contract. Would there be a realistic chance of that being extended?'

You're likely to have non-committal replies, but rarely will you be told straight out not to bother applying, and that ought to be good enough to encourage you to apply.

However, a head teacher I spoke to adds a note of caution here: 'Application packs are carefully put together, and the school won't take too kindly to questions that merely show you haven't read them properly.'

ANNOUNCE YOUR INTENTIONS AT THE RIGHT TIME

There are some jobs where you can walk into work one morning, pick up your stuff and tell the manager you're off to something better, goodbye. Teaching is not like that. The leadership will find out soon enough that you're planning to leave, and the news should come from you first.

If you are open with your colleagues about looking for jobs (and you don't have to be if you don't want to), then the leadership will soon pick up on it, and you may think it is polite to discuss your plans with them as soon as you start talking in the staffroom. In a well-run school, where leaders are genuinely interested in the progress of their colleagues, you may well find excellent advice and additional insights from talks with your head and other leaders. This can sometimes be necessarily frank: 'I'm very happy to support you with that job, but I don't think you're ready for the other one.'

A head says: 'Speak with your head *before* you even apply – ask their advice and think about the timing. The school will need to replace you if you are successful – don't do it in the last week or so of the "window".'

In any case, you must tell the leadership once you've started visiting other schools and filling in applications, because you don't want your head to find out from a third party, perhaps at a meeting or from a reference request.

Some people are embarrassed about telling the leadership team that they're going to leave. There's no need to be.

Remember:

- You aren't the centre of the universe.
- Over the years every head sees dozens, maybe hundreds, of teachers come and go.
- The earlier your leaders know you might be leaving, and need to be replaced, the better.
- If you're ambitious and excellent, people expect you to move on.
- Many good leaders will support staff in moving their careers on.
- You need a reference from your current head anyway, and it's deeply discourteous not to ask first.

LINE UP YOUR REFEREES IN ADVANCE

Website chat among teachers shows lots of misunderstanding about this point.

Here's what a teacher wrote on a website forum: 'I sent out the application form and they rang my school for a reference the morning they got the form, just as I was going to tell the head.' This is a teacher who didn't know the essential rule, which is: ask your chosen referees, *before* you write them on the form, if they are willing to provide references.

This is an important part of your preparation to apply for a job. Anyone who is accustomed to being asked for a reference will tell you that it's not a responsibility ever taken on lightly. So ask your desired referees properly, either in writing or in a semi-formal meeting (not in a corridor encounter). Show them the details of the job (or attach them if you're asking by post or email). Don't take it for granted that they will agree. Refusals have been known.

WHO SHOULD YOU ASK TO BE REFEREES?

A student teacher will give the training institution as his/her first referee. If you're already working in a school, whether as a qualified teacher or on a long-term placement, you must give your current head. There's no acceptable reason for not doing so. If you don't name your head, it raises questions and the panel may contact them anyway.

A second referee will probably be your head of department and a third, if it's needed, the head of a previous school if it's not too long ago. It's better to leave the third referee blank than to give an essentially meaningless one, such as a family friend.

HOW REFERENCES ARE USED

There's misunderstanding about this, too. In many areas of work, references are taken up after the job offer, which is made 'subject to satisfactory references'. In teaching, however, the offer is often made on the day of the interview, so references are usually called in earlier in the process.

The usual practices are:

- If there are only a few applications, everybody's references might be taken up.

- If there are lots of applications, references might be taken up for promising candidates as part of the initial sorting, producing what's sometimes called 'the long list' (as opposed to the 'shortlist' of candidates to be interviewed).

- Quite often, only the references of shortlisted candidates are taken up. In either case, if you discover that your referees have been approached, it's usually a sign that your application has at least not been summarily thrown out because you used green ink or had a porridge stain on the form.

Bear in mind, though, that many teachers place more importance on written references than is justified. References are necessarily confined to factual confirmation of your own claim of suitability for the post. They will not conflict with what's on your performance record and they will not contain gossip or unsubstantiated opinion. Here are two paragraphs from a typical advice document on references which one UK local authority sends to heads and governors:

> All information given in a reference should be based on fact. Head teachers should be cautious about giving any subjective opinion about an individual's performance, conduct or suitability, which cannot be verified with factual evidence.
>
> Head teachers may be asked to express an opinion about an employee's capabilities, skills or personal qualities. Head teachers can answer these types of questions, but they must ensure that their comments are based upon personal knowledge and observation of the individual.

This caution, which includes the fact that references are kept in case of future disputes, stems from concern for the teacher's rights under employment law. As a result, unless a reference reveals a dishonest application, it will not usually change an appointing panel's judgement, although it may confirm their line of thought.

Sometimes, heads are approached to give references over the phone. It's not an acceptable practice, and heads are advised not to do it.

One head says, of the whole reference system: 'I worked with a chair of governors who openly said that references were effectively worthless. That's certainly not correct, but what I will say is that references are rarely as important as the candidates think they are.'

KEY POINTS

- Find out everything you possibly can about your desired job.
- Do not be swayed by sentiment or 'grass is greener' feelings.
- Be courteous in your dealings with your senior leadership team (SLT) and colleagues.
- Be realistic about the importance of references.

GOOD TEACHERS MAKE GOOD SCHOOL VISITORS

GOOD TEACHERS MAKE GOOD SCHOOL VISITORS

IF YOU'RE SERIOUS, YOU'LL VISIT

Some schools positively encourage visits. Very few positively discourage them. This sentence from a real job advertisement tells you why: 'Please feel free to come to visit the school prior to application, as this will show you why we are so proud of what St Paul's is all about and give you an idea of what you could offer to our community.'

There are three potential windows of opportunity for a visit:

1 Before you even apply.

2 When you've been invited to interview.

3 On the interview day itself.

Ideally you'll go for Window 1. Yes, it can be difficult to accomplish – distance, travel costs, your own work commitments all get in the way. But if the advert and the details they send are starting to convince you – particularly if they go out of their way to encourage visits – then it's worth making a real effort to see the place and spend significant time there, and in the neighbourhood. Doing this while there's still time to reflect on the experience will help you decide whether or not to apply. If you go ahead, you will do so armed with valuable information and mental images that you will bear in mind throughout the application process. If the visit is a disappointment, you will be saved a good deal of time and trouble. Importantly, too, seeing the place will remove any 'maybe I should have applied' feelings.

Window 2 is the next best. You've already passed a hurdle by reaching the shortlist. The visit, if you use it properly, will arm you for the interview.

Window 3 is the fall-back option. It's almost certain there will be a tour of the school on the interview day. If you have to settle for that, study the interview day programme closely to ensure that you're going to get a good look around. Contact the school if it's not clear.

You may have the opportunity to use two of those opportunities, even all three. But be careful how you handle that. If they see you three times, will they be cumulatively more impressed by your enthusiasm and personality each time? Or will they say, 'Not her again'? Maybe it would be best to stay well in the background on one of the three.

But whenever you make your visit, be aware that it's important for two basic reasons. One is obvious, which is to enable you to take a good look at the school; the other is sometimes overlooked, which is to let the school have a preliminary look at you.

So let's deal with both of those.

WHAT ARE YOU LOOKING FOR?

Essentially, it's simple. 'Is this the job for me, in a place where I want to spend my working life?' Much will depend on your own expectations for the job, but here's a basic checklist of things to keep alert for.

- **Rowdy classrooms.** Any school can have pockets of ill-discipline, but most classrooms should look and sound purposeful and orderly.

- **Wandering children** in lesson time. Corridors should be quiet during lessons. If you're with any member of staff, teacher or not, they should be checking any child found on the loose.

- **Children you meet in corridors and shared areas**, especially between lessons, should be orderly and self-controlled, and certainly not intimidating to a visitor. If there's a break or lunchtime gathering ground or common area it should show children at their best – lively, laughing, joking, polite to passing adults, relaxed and smiling. (Sneering, whispered remarks or insolent stares are not good signals of a school's health.)

- **Staff are welcoming.** If, as so often, you have to wait in the entrance area when you arrive, do passing staff smile? Does anyone ask, 'Are you being looked after?' Or do they hurry past without a glance? Are you invited into the staffroom at break? What sort of reception do you find there? What's the atmosphere like?

- **Litter.** Some schools have a blind spot for litter and chewing gum stains, which look terrible to a visitor.

- **Smelly toilets – one for the nose.** It's really difficult to keep toilets, especially boys', smelling sweet, but some schools manage it, and it gives an indication of the importance the school places on the learning and working environment.

- **Feeling comfortable.** Some schools just generally make you feel comfortable – staff looking after you are not distracted, and you are in no hurry to leave. Other schools seem to give off a feeling of tension, as if there has to be constant vigilance and control, and there's little spare energy for just being … well, nice is the word.

THE NEIGHBOURHOOD

Find out where most of the children come from, and take a look around. Walking is best, but the size of the area may mean driving or diverting your taxi. Incidentally, one advantage of being in a taxi is that you usually have another source of background information about the area. (But remember, it's a possibly biased one-person sample.)

If you'll have to move house, this may be the time for an initial look at where you might live.

ASK THE RIGHT QUESTIONS

Don't just walk around the school vacantly nodding and smiling. Glean information as you go. If you still haven't applied, this is an opportunity to get answers that weren't in the printed information. Write them down ahead of time and check them off.

For example, if you haven't cleared up any of the following (if you've reached the interview stage, you probably should have), then tick off as many as possible on your school visit.

■ The exact demands of the job.   ☐

- ■ Its place in the hierarchy, and the salary structure. ☐
- ■ The rooms you would be working in. ☐
- ■ What your office is like (if it's that kind of job). ☐
- ■ What admin/technical support will be available to you. ☐
- ■ What the teaching load is likely to be. ☐
- ■ Who you will be teaching alongside. ☐

Not all the answers will be available – some will be decided after your appointment – but they're reasonable questions to ask. Broached politely and conversationally, not assertively, in the context of a guided tour, they show the seriousness of your intentions.

ON SHOW FROM THE WORD GO

We've already said that a visit also lets people in the school have a look at you. Whenever and however you visit a school to which you might apply or already have applied, you are under scrutiny, so present yourself well. I'll say more about this in the chapter on interviews, page 121. Meanwhile, here's what one very successful and experienced academy principal says:

First impressions really do matter – making sure you speak in a polite and friendly manner to all staff/students encountered throughout the day. We regularly receive feedback from our reception team, when they are impressed by the way a candidate has signed in or said goodbye, and I always find out from my PA what he thought about them.

Did you not realise that sort of thing went on? You do now.

AFTER THE VISIT

Study your notes and go through the visit in your mind. Make a list of pros and cons. Do the same for other visits so you can make comparisons. Consider some of the practicalities – driving distances, public transport, house prices, your children's schooling, your partner's work. Above all, *stay grounded*. It's easy to be carried away into the wrong decision. It's just one school, one job, one town. There's always another.

KEY POINTS

- Remember that the people showing you their school want you to be impressed.

- Be frank about things you see that worry you – there may be good explanations.

- If you're taken in for school lunch, ask to sit with some students.

- If you go into a classroom, take notice of how the children react to a visitor.

GOOD TEACHERS MAKE GOOD JOB APPLICATIONS

GOOD TEACHERS MAKE GOOD JOB APPLICATIONS

You've checked the closing date, know the terms of your existing contract, and lined up your referees. Now it's time to sit down and commit yourself on paper. First, though, reflect on the fact that *brilliance is not enough*.

The guiding principle which should stay with all job candidates from start to finish is: *It's not about you, it's about the job, and whether you can do it.*

Obviously, the school – the head, recruitment panel, governors – will all be looking at you with interest, trying to assess your qualities. But they are not seeing you in shining isolated brilliance.

They are seeing you in context, judging you in relationship to the place they are trying to fill. Ultimately, their job is to ensure that students are well taught, respected and safe, and they want someone who fits that bill. All of this is a long way from, 'How brilliant is this applicant?'

What this means in practice is that while it's OK to go on about how wonderful you are, it's vital to ensure that you focus on the qualities that will enable you to excel at the advertised post.

SELL YOURSELF

Why do you think you are writing the application? Why, in the hope of getting the job, of course. What else?

In fact, the purpose is more immediate and has three aims, which are:

1 **To get an interview.** You won't get the job unless you're interviewed, so that's what you must keep in mind. It means you sell yourself hard on the application, and don't leave anything to be taken for granted. Beware, particularly, of thinking, 'I needn't put that in. I'll leave it for the interview.' Many applicants do exactly that, clearly having failed to engage their brains properly.

2 **To get the panel feeling good about you before they meet you.** A good application actually biases the panel – they brighten up at the thought of seeing you. You want someone – preferably an influential member of the recruitment panel – to read your application and say, 'I like the look of this one!' In the most fortunate of circumstances, the job becomes yours to lose. And, believe me, you certainly can lose it.

3 **To keep the job if you land it.** That means being honest and not covering up any gaps in your record, or massaging your qualifications (more of this later; see page 84).

So handle the whole application process with the greatest of care. It's a tightrope: one foot wrong and you will tumble to your doom. An article in *The Guardian* in 2013 by senior teacher Alan Newland described how a head teacher did a first 'sift' of applications by looking for spelling mistakes: 'If people can't even be bothered to use a spell checker, let alone proofread their own application form,' she said, 'then they don't really want to work here. I'm not denying them the opportunity of a job. They're ruling themselves out'.[1]

That, however, is only part of the story. The process really begins when you make your first contact with the school to which you intend to apply. Suppose there's something in the information for applicants that you need to check. Can you call the school to ask about it? Of course. But, first, avoid looking foolish by making doubly sure that the answer is not already there in the sheaf of information you've been sent. Then, when you do call, be sure you're polite and pleasant. You want the person on the other end, whoever it is, to put the phone down and say, 'He/she sounds like a sensible person.'

---

1   Alan Newland. 'To bin or not to bin: how headteachers sift job applications', *The Guardian* (January 2013). Available at: http://www.theguardian.com/teacher-network/teacher-blog/2013/jan/10/teaching-job-applications-rejected-headteachers.

YOU CAN'T PUT IT OFF ANY LONGER

Now it's time to sit down to compose the application. There are two related tasks. One is to fill in the official form. The other is to write the supporting statement or letter of application (various terms are used).

Sometimes there's space on the form for the letter, but even so I'd say always do it on a separate document.

If the form and letter are hard copy:

- Make two or three photocopies of the form before you start.
- Do your first draft of everything in pencil. That one's just for you.
- Use black ink if it says so – it's because they'll be making photocopies.
- Keep tidy, write neatly within the boxes. Don't cross out; start again.
- Number pages, and put your name on every page.

THE FORM

Two cast-iron principles apply here – accuracy and honesty.

ACCURACY

A typical form is generic, which means you may have to fill in the name of the school, and almost certainly the title of the post for which you're applying. *Get these right in every detail.* Many applicants fall at this hurdle. More than you'd think submit applications with the name of the school wrongly spelled. This can lead to an application being binned unread. Get all the details – is there an apostrophe in there somewhere? Is the word 'The' included ('The Perse School')? Are there extra words such as 'Academy' or 'Community' or 'Collegiate'?

Equally importantly, make sure you spell the head's name correctly, and use the correct title: are you sure it's Mr? Might it be Dr?

Final check – if you are making more than one application, be 100 per cent certain that the right one is going to the right school. Take a moment to rehearse the chill that will go through your bones when you realise you've got that one wrong.

The same attention to detail must go through the whole of the application form. Get the names of your previous schools and posts correct, and the titles of your qualifications.

Don't overload the application form. List jobs by title, most recent first. Don't provide a cricket score of CPD courses – mention the most significant and recent that are relevant to your application.

HONESTY

The application form is a key document that is scrutinised and checked by the appropriate department – usually human resources – of your new employers. So, fill in all of the form. Each question is there for a reason. If any clearly does not apply to you, say so, and why. If you want clarification, call and ask. Give accurate dates and correct titles and grades for your previous jobs, and correct details of your degrees and other relevant qualifications.

Teachers have lost jobs through deliberate massaging of applications; for example, by:

- Upgrading a degree or modifying its title to fit the subject you're hoping to teach.
- Tweaking your present job title and description so it looks either more senior than it really is, or more relevant to the job you're seeking.

In one real example, a teacher who had left a job after only a few unhappy weeks felt that the episode looked bad on his applications and was sure that was why he was failing to get promotion. Frustrated, on his next attempt he covered up the short stay by simply leaving it off his form and 'stretching' the time he had spent in the previous job.

This time he was successful, and he was interviewed and appointed. The human resources (HR) department, however, discovered the truth after he'd started work – and he was dismissed.

In industry, an excellent applicant who was performing impressively in the new job might just find a sympathetic listener and get away with that particular bit of chicanery. In education, though, quite apart from the dishonesty, the highly practical and sensitive issue of the safeguarding of children is involved, and no employment gaps can be tolerated, especially if they're deliberately covered up. So be prepared for a panel member to go through your service record with you in detail. If you've lied on the form, you'll then have to look him or her in the eye and lie again. You will not get away with it, and you may well damage your whole future.

THE LETTER OF APPLICATION

This, really, is the key document. Take your time over it, but that doesn't mean it needs to be long. About one side of A4, and never more than two, is the aim. Of course, all spelling, grammar and factual information must be totally accurate, and the layout has to be tidy, professional and business-like, but not fancy. It isn't a Christmas round robin. Fancy fonts, pretty borders, irrelevant logos and emoticons are irritating and can suggest that you don't understand what's appropriate. Sheer sloppiness is often taken as a sign that you don't want the job badly enough.

Here are some basic rules about content.

Address your letter of application to the head, using his or her name. It's not difficult to find it – it will usually be on the school website. Spell it correctly; use the title 'Dear Dr Johnson' or 'Dear Sir Robert' if it's appropriate. (NB It's not 'Dear Sir Robert Smith', and there's no full stop after Dr or after Mr/Mrs.) Avoid 'Dear Sir or Madam' because this says, 'I couldn't be bothered to find out your name', or 'I'm sending the same basic letter, with a few tweaks, to seven other schools', or both.

All the way through, keep the letter focused on their job. Keep the person specification by you – open on the same screen if you can – and make sure everything you write is relevant to it. If it helps, use section headings based on the person specification. (Incidentally, if the school advertises more than one job, don't apply for more than one of them. It smacks of desperation.)

Write your own letter, separately and individually, for each job. This means you cannot try to make one letter work for several jobs by cutting and pasting. It's lazy and easily spotted. Neither can you copy someone else's brilliant letter, or a sample letter you've seen on a website. There are two reasons for this.

First, I know that heads sometimes receive the identical letter from more than one candidate. That's almost inevitable given that friendship groups of teachers and student teachers often work together on applications, but it's almost bound to result in both letters being binned.

Second, any kind of shared letter must, by definition, be too generic, whereas a good letter is specifically targeted on the job and the school.

The advice from heads is, by all means look at each other's applications, but only for inspiration. After the sharing and the discussion, put everything aside and write your own.

When you think you're finished, go through and see if you can weed out as many uses of 'I' or 'my' as you can. Overuse can seem boastful – centred on you rather than on the job.

Then do a final spellcheck, using UK software.

Finally, send off the application. Check how to do this – quite often you're asked to send it both electronically and as hard copy in the post. Either way, keep and file an electronic copy.

WHAT ABOUT A CV?

A CV (curriculum vitae – sometimes called résumé) is a generic summary of your career, not aimed at a particular audience. It is useful to have one and keep it up to date as a personal reminder of key dates and events, but it's hardly ever requested in connection with a teaching job application. The completed form and a personal statement add up to enough information. Heads will tell you, in weary resignation, that this doesn't stop candidates from sending their CVs, sometimes illustrated with not very relevant photographs and even PowerPoint presentations. For this reason, the application pack sometimes contains the pointed instruction, 'Please do NOT send a CV.'

KEY POINTS

- Writing applications is onerous and time-consuming – make time and space to do it properly.

- Create as many drafts as you need before you're satisfied.

- Focus on the job, and your suitability for it.

- Have a last careful read before you send the application off.

GOOD TEACHERS UNDERSTAND HOW INTERVIEWS WORK

GOOD TEACHERS UNDERSTAND HOW INTERVIEWS WORK

Now let's assume you're called for interview, by letter, email or phone call. Usually there's a sensible amount of notice, but it's not unusual to have very little. You can allow yourself to feel good at this point, because you're clearly seen as a viable candidate, on paper at least. Now's the time to begin making sure you don't give away this advantage.

The job interview is a standard recruitment tool. Its imperfections are well known – a good interview does not necessarily translate to a good job performance. (Just type 'Interviews don't work' into a search engine and you'll see what I mean.) That's why, in teaching, the selection/recruitment committee will also be influenced by some or all of a number of other factors – the written application, the demonstration lesson, the presentation to the panel, the children's interview, the general impression made on a school visit, references, and, inevitably, any further information that the panel has on the candidate (if he or she is already working at the school, for example).

It's at the final, formal interview, though, where the appointment decision is made. That's where gut feelings can come into play, and unexpectedly courageous (or foolhardy) decisions are occasionally made – to appoint a relatively inexperienced enthusiast perhaps, or to reject a favoured internal candidate. Schools, local authorities and academy trusts have all developed their own approach to the interview process, so do not take the following description as a universal template. There may well be significant differences in detail and structure between schools and organisations. In the end, however, the principle is always the same: a group of the school's decision-makers – usually senior leaders and governors – come together to identify, through face-to-face question and answer, the person best suited to their job and their institution.

THE GROUND RULES

Usually, each member of the interview panel has a hard copy of each candidate's application documents – form, letter, references. They will also have either attended, or had reported to them, the candidate's demonstration lesson, presentation and, if it happened, interview by the students.

Diligent interviewers will have studied all of this material. Much of the questioning will be informed by the documents, and will consist of probing for evidence to support statements and opinions. At least one member of the panel may take the candidate point-by-point through his or her list of jobs to be sure there are no unexplained or covered-up gaps. Some panel members may not have studied the documents quite so diligently, if at all, and their questions sometimes reflect that.

PREPARED QUESTIONS

Interview panels prepare questions carefully, because employment law, safe recruitment practice and basic principles of fair play need to be observed. They may well be advised on this by an HR professional – perhaps (especially if a new head is being recruited) to the extent of having done a bespoke recruitment course.

The panel will normally agree in advance on a core set of questions, which are distributed around the panel. The head and the head of department will be strongly influential in choosing these topics, but other panel members should always take the opportunity to address their own priorities and interests. Because questions are prepared with particular aims in view they can sound stilted or scripted, and sometimes be difficult to understand. Panel members are free to follow up on the answers to questions, and it is at this stage where an interview can begin to flow freely or bump into a series of awkward misunderstandings on either side.

WHO DOES THE INTERVIEWING?

There's no quick answer to this. In most schools, appointments are made by the governing body, who will usually appoint a recruitment/appointment committee with full delegated powers. This committee, unless the appointment is for a new head, will include the head teacher, probably other senior staff with relevant expertise, and perhaps an outside adviser or a consultant from the local authority. Whether all members of the recruitment committee form the actual panel for every interview or not is up to them. They may well all be there for a senior appointment, or they may delegate the appointment to a much smaller group, perhaps including the head, a subject or department leader and one governor.

In most cases the head will have a very strong voice in the ultimate choice, but other members often exercise their influence, and those being interviewed would do well to remember that.

BE READY FOR THE FORMALITY

One teacher I spoke to said:

> For my first and second teaching jobs, in primary schools, I was interviewed only by the head with one governor who said little. They weren't like interviews at all. For one of them, I was the only candidate, and the head was making me a cup of tea as he talked to me. I think they were glad to get a reasonable candidate – it was late in the summer holidays, with term starting in a week or two, and I was always going to get the job as long as I lived up to my letter of application.

Then after some years, I was interviewed for the deputy headship of a big primary in the city. I was thrown when I walked into the room. My memory tells me there were about fifteen people facing me across a big table. That can't be right. There must only have been half a dozen at most. But it gives you an idea of how I felt.

They all spoke formally, and the ones that weren't speaking to me would watch me closely and then bend their heads to scribble down some notes. I knew who the head was, because I'd already met her, but I didn't know any of the others. The chair introduced everyone, but I quickly forgot everything she said, so I had no idea who was asking me what and why.

I really had problems handling it. I forgot simple stuff, and I went away kicking myself that I'd not made enough of my experience and abilities. I didn't get that job, but by golly it was a learning experience and I was ready for the next interview, which I had soon afterwards, with a better outcome.

SAFEGUARDING AND CHILD PROTECTION

At least one member of the panel will probably be trained in safe recruitment practice, and among the prepared questions there will always be one or more about safeguarding and child protection. It may be couched in terms of, 'What would you do if …?' or, 'Can you give an example of when you've been concerned about …'

However, it's often said that 'safeguarding' is more a matter of a teacher's appropriate attitude and approach to, than knowledge of, written guidelines, and so questions might be quite subtle. At least one panel member will be looking, throughout the interview, for evidence of how you approach child protection.

THE PANEL IS MADE UP OF INDIVIDUALS

Throughout the interview, each member of the panel will have his or her own unspoken priorities.

For example:

■ **Parent governor:**

'Can I see this person teaching my child?'

■ **Head:**

'Is this person a good and committed enough teacher to support my drive for overall improvement?'

■ **Department head:**

'How will this person fit in with my carefully built team?'

■ **Educational consultant, adviser or inspector:**

'Is this someone who can help address some of our concerns about this school?'

■ **Long-serving governor:**

'Is this someone who will understand our community and be welcomed by the local people?'

That's a simplification, of course. Experienced interviewers try hard to take a broad view of their responsibilities. And here's what one head said: 'I always sit through an interview thinking, "Would I want this person to teach my children?" I imagine most heads with children would think this. The other thing I think is, "Will this person fit in with the school ethos and the rest of the school team?"'

An interview panel is made up of a diverse collection of people, with ideas that sometimes go off in unexpected directions, and candidates need to be alert for curve-ball questions. Some questions, indeed, betray differences of philosophy within the panel – for example, about much-debated subjects such as how best to teach reading and whether or not to set by ability. You need to be good at framing diplomatic, tightrope-walking answers to much of what you're asked.

KEY POINTS

- Keep in mind that the interview is where the final decision is made.
- The structure is likely to be formal and well prepared.
- The panel may include 'lay' people with different kinds of experience.

GOOD TEACHERS PREPARE
WELL FOR INTERVIEWS

GOOD TEACHERS PREPARE WELL FOR INTERVIEWS

If you're called for interview, it shows that you're a viable candidate. Interviewing candidates is a serious and time-consuming business for a school and they are not interested in including people just to make up numbers.

It follows that you will take the invitation in the same spirit of professionalism by responding properly to it and preparing meticulously. Any sign that you are underprepared or lacking in commitment can destroy your chances.

PRELIMINARY HOUSEKEEPING

First, make sure that you have the *correct, double-checked date and time* firmly fixed in your mind, in your diary, and maybe on a pin board in your home. If there is any apparent ambiguity in the invitation (the date is on a Sunday, or the given time seems to be in the late evening) then check with the school. Mistakes do happen, and you don't need any nagging uncertainties.

Similarly, *be sure you know where the interview will take place*. You're assuming it's at the school, but read the letter carefully in case you find, in a sentence right at the bottom, 'All interviews will take place at the county education offices, 22 High Street'. (In that case, as we've already established, you really need to be sure that you see the school before you're interviewed.)

Check, too, *whether the interview is a whole-day or a two-day process*. If it's over two days, there's likely to be a weeding out of candidates at the end of day one, but of course you will assume in advance that you'll need to clear your diary for both days.

Take time to consider *how you will get there*. You cannot risk being late. No matter how good your excuse and how soothing the receptionist, if you arrive late you start off uncomfortable and rushed. Check all the travelling options, and do a dry run if possible. If there's any doubt, plan for an overnight stay. If you're driving and the letter fails to mention parking, consider asking about it, because in many schools it's very limited and you don't want to start the day off badly by chasing frantically around looking for a parking space.

Get your interview clothes and hair sorted. Don't wake up on I-Day morning and discover that a key garment is un-ironed, your preferred shoes are covered in mud and you really should have visited the hairdresser two days ago.

Put together a portfolio? There's a question mark here because not all experienced interviewers feel that a portfolio is necessary. The answer is probably to put one together if you have work or photographs that have a direct bearing on your application, but don't produce them unless the opportunity is fairly obvious, and even then only after asking permission. In any case, don't take a whole heap of stuff.

If you are taking other necessary materials with you, for a demonstration lesson or presentation, double- and treble-check everything well in advance. Write a checklist and tape it where it's always visible – the kitchen work surface, for example.

(I cover preparing the content of a demonstration lesson and/or a presentation to the panel separately; see pages 133 and 143.)

READ THROUGH YOUR APPLICATION FORM AND LETTER

You may well have written your application some time ago, and have possibly written others in the meantime. (You do have copies, of course.) Study everything you wrote in detail, because some interview panel members will lean heavily on these materials as a source of questions. If you've made an assertion, can you back it up from experience? If you did an unusual job, do you have something interesting to say about it? Avoid being caught obviously having forgotten what you wrote in your own letter. Leaning across and saying, 'I organised a trip where, did you say? Can I just look at that for a moment? My, my, well, I never,' is not likely to go down well.

MENTAL HOUSEKEEPING

You're a busy person. Your days are full. You know the interview is approaching, but do not let it arrive and catch you unprepared. Take time shortly beforehand to declutter your thoughts and do a mental audit of your personal qualities and your fitness for the job. As you do so, think of examples of your work which both demonstrate each point and are also relevant to the school and job you are applying for.

For example:

- I'm confident and successful in the classroom.
- I get on well with colleagues.
- I am supportive and sympathetic to less experienced colleagues.
- I am respected by parents and colleagues.
- I enjoy the company of children.
- I am professional, diligent and honest.
- I am proud to carry the title 'teacher'.
- I have skills that I know other people do not have.

Then *write down the key messages you want to transmit to the interviewer*, which say, 'I am the person you are looking for.'

- ■ I have good experience in the area you're looking for.
- ■ I have the right qualifications.
- ■ I am accustomed to working in a team like the one you have in mind.
- ■ I have the necessary subject knowledge and classroom skills.
- ■ I have made good progress in my career so far and am well equipped to continue.

Now go through these and add a note for each to remind you of a specific example or occasion of how (in school, in your work) you have demonstrated that quality. Do this, study the results, and add to it as you think of better examples.

SUBJECT KNOWLEDGE

In many cases, the schools to which you apply will take it for granted that you know enough about your subject – that if you're applying to teach geography, you actually know lots about geography. Your degree and other qualifications may well make that a reasonable assumption.

However, there's evidence that some school leaders and heads of department are not prepared to take subject knowledge for granted. They know that the content of an A level course, for example, will call for a particular collection of concepts and facts that you may not even have touched on in a degree course.

One physics teacher told me: 'In my interview I was grilled on what I knew about the content of the A level physics course, and I'm pretty sure I got the job over other candidates because I was able to answer the questions well.' So, be prepared. If you're applying to teach a specialist subject to exam level, be as sure as you can that you would pass the exam yourself if you had to take it.

KNOWLEDGE OF TEACHING AND LEARNING

However, as well as your own experience, you will need to be certain of your knowledge of current thinking and events insofar as they relate to the job. Be ready for the questions. Read the specialist press, comb the internet for articles relating to your subject and the job, and be aware of relevant high-profile books and reports. Right up to the morning of the interview, be alert for media announcements which may come up at the interview, or which you can mention yourself. Be particularly aware of the place and importance of information and communications technology (ICT) in the job you're applying for.

Your overall aim is to be well prepared for the interview, as quietly relaxed and confident as a pianist who knows the concerto he is about to play thoroughly and well in every nuance.

Finally, don't forget:

It's not about *you*. It's about their job and whether you can do it.

KEY POINTS

■ Set aside time to think about your interview.

■ Have a mock interview, if possible, with someone experienced.

■ Video yourself talking as if to an interview panel.

GOOD TEACHERS ARE READY FOR INTERVIEW DAY

It's interview day. You've arrived on time and had a tour of the school. You've taught a lesson to a class and made a brief presentation to a panel which might be made up of the same people as will carry out your formal interview. In many schools you will also have met, or been interviewed by, a representative group of children. Each of these we deal with separately.

Now you face, towards the end of the day – in some cases, at the end of a two-day process – the formal decisive interview.

By now you've already made a significant impression on the panel. They think they know you pretty well, after your written application, your prepared lesson and your presentation. It may be that the job is now yours – so long as you do not insult the chair, recite 'Eskimo Nell', take a call from your bookie or laugh maniacally as you remove items of your clothing.

Or the reverse may be the case. You may have gone down so badly up to now that you face an uphill task.

But – and this is important – there is no point trying to guess because there's every chance that you will guess wrongly, and good panel members certainly give nothing away. They take their responsibility more seriously than that. Nobody, for example, is going to give you a thumbs-up behind the others' backs after your presentation.

Any apparent sense of where you stand at any point before the final decision is likely to be wrong, and you must put it aside.

Experienced advertising executive, Jeremy Bullmore, puts his finger on the reason for this in his advice column. Dealing with an enquirer who feels badly served by interview, he makes the crucial point that no interviewee can judge his or her performance against that of other candidates. Only the interviewers can do that, as they try to find the person best fitted for the post. 'The only comparisons the interviewee can make are with other interviews that he or she has already experienced.'[1]

Whether you feel you've done well, or badly, in any individual interview (or any part of the selection process), this bears no relation to the only comparisons that really matter, which are the ones being made between candidates by the selection panel, and of which you can know nothing.

So, *go through the day assuming that at any point all the way to the end there is everything to play for.*

A TYPICAL INTERVIEW DAY ITINERARY

Physical on-the-day arrangements vary considerably. Here's just one way the day can go.

---

1 Jeremy Bullmore. 'Dear Jeremy – your work issues solved', *The Guardian*, (January 2015). Available at: http://www.theguardian.com/money/2015/jan/17/job-interview-used-management-free-work-gym-trainer.

- All the candidates (between three and six) arrive at the same time in the morning and are made welcome with coffee. A member of staff explains the day, and then takes them on a tour of the school.

- All the candidates have lunch, perhaps with staff or children.

- The candidates are put in a waiting room and are called for interview one at a time. After their interview they either leave, to be phoned later, or they return to the waiting room.

- After the last interview, the panel discusses its decision.

- The successful candidate is offered the job, either on the phone or after being called back to the interview room.

- The others receive a word of encouragement and perhaps the offer of a formal debrief, and off they go to phone their ever-supportive families.

In addition, candidates are frequently asked to teach a lesson, and often also give a presentation to the interview panel on a given topic relevant to the job. They may also meet a group of children for an encounter that may or may not be called an interview. An elaborate timetable will cycle the candidates through these stages.

Candidates for senior posts may also have to do an 'in-tray exercise' (see page 151).

Also common, especially for senior posts, is the two-stage 'knockout' where the first interview is used by the panel to select a shortlist for the second interview.

The process is draining and calls for considerable physical and emotional stamina, so you should go into it well fed, well rested, bright-eyed and bushy-tailed.

On the day, when you're getting ready at home, feeling nervous, this is where your written notes and checklists come into play. Be methodical, give yourself time and do not leave home until you are sure you have everything you need.

THE BASICS

BE PUNCTUAL

Obviously you won't be late, but neither should you be awkwardly early. The school has its own timetable for the day and early arrivals will simply have to wait, often under the inscrutable gaze of the reception staff.

DRESS

Dress really is important. More and more secondary schools are insisting on jacket and tie uniforms for their students, with primaries following a little less formally. At the same time, staff are often expected to adopt business-style working clothes. If you've done your homework and kept your eyes open on your preliminary visit, you'll know what you need to buy, beg, borrow or unearth for your visit and interview. Don't try to convince yourself that 'If they really want me they'll take me as I am'. It won't work. Remember you're dealing with lay governors as well as professionals.

So, dress for business – conservatively, modestly, thoughtfully and extremely well. But in any case, make sure your clothes are clean, of reasonable quality and well pressed. Wear decent shoes, and if you can polish them, make them gleam. Some interviewers judge everyone they meet by their shoes – or, I'm told, their socks. Generally, aim for an air of fresh and classy simplicity.

Sort out anything that will give trouble before you leave home (trousers slipping down, underwear scrunching up, collar itching, tights laddered, fly zip unreliable (the ultimate horror)). If you look the part, you'll feel right and be comfortable among the other candidates.

ATTITUDE

Right from the start, when you enter the building, be pleasant and polite to everyone. Much more than you think is fed back to the interviewers as the day goes on. Give firm but not bone-crushing handshakes, and introduce yourself clearly, without mumbling. Make eye contact, keep your hands out of your pockets.

Take care to be pleasant and responsive to children you meet, but not over-fussy in a 'look how good I am with children' kind of way. If you're being conducted around by a member of staff, they'll notice well enough how you genuinely relate to children and will feed their impressions back.

GROUP BEHAVIOUR

Interviewees for teaching jobs are usually called all at the same time, and kept as a group when they are not individually required. The whole group may be conducted around on a tour, and be on semi-public view in other situations such as at lunch.

Be very aware that there's almost always someone who, in the group setting, sets out to impress either the rest of the group or any observing members of staff, or both. Make sure it's not you, because it's counterproductive. Here's a teacher reminiscing about someone she knew:

All the heads in our small town knew Jack, because they'd all had him on interview at some time. He was notorious for appearing to be loud and obnoxious when he was with other candidates and on tours of the school – boasting about how well he knew the school and how experienced he was at his specialism. It was a real shame, because underneath he was OK, good with children and hard-working. It was nervousness, I guess, and a fear of being ignored. He always wondered why he didn't get jobs, and, sadly, none of the interviewing heads had the courage to be frank with him about his attitude. They just passed him over.

On the whole, if you want to impress, do it by being generally quiet, polite and self-contained. Laugh, but not uproariously, when it's appropriate. Stand to speak to someone who's already standing. Don't fidget.

Lastly – and this is very important: *do not take or make calls or check your phone at any point during interview day*. It ought not to be necessary to make this point, but there are many stories of job candidates taking and making calls during interviews. If you're desperate – terminally ill mother, partner about to give birth, lottery numbers apparently matching – go in the toilet to make your call. Even then, the deputy head will probably come in just as you're amusing your partner by imitating his or her accent.

MEETING CHILDREN FORMALLY

The practice of asking interview candidates to meet, or be interviewed by, a group of children, perhaps the school council, is increasingly common in both primary and secondary schools.

They will take the task very seriously, and ask carefully prepared questions, making notes of the answers. It's possible that they may have no follow-up questions, so you will need to help things along.

For your part, take the process seriously, but be relaxed and try to maintain the kind of conversation that you might have on any day in your own school. Ask them questions – what do they like about their school? Smile a lot, be courteous and kind. (Children always mention 'kindness' as a key teacher quality.) Include them all, even if one or two dominate.

The group will give feedback to the school leadership, perhaps indirectly through their own teacher. The detail of what they say may be less important than their general impression, which should be: 'This is someone we'd like as our teacher.'

THE DAY WORKS BOTH WAYS

You may arrive on interview day convinced you'll be devastated if you don't get the job. Try to dispense with that feeling and be as dispassionate and objective as you can. If you start to have negative feelings, reflect on them and identify where they're coming from. The whole day is a two-way process and it may end with your withdrawal from the interview. This is not unusual or shameful, and it does not show any kind of weakness on your part. It will be respected by the school – they would rather you withdrew now, rather than them end up employing someone who feels they've done the wrong thing.

KEY POINTS

- Arrive punctually, looking smart and pleasant.
- Throughout the day, be professionally interested in the children's work.
- Be quiet, but ready with relevant and incisive questions.
- Use the time to confirm whether or not the school is for you.

GOOD TEACHERS ARE GOOD AT INTERVIEWS

GOOD TEACHERS ARE GOOD AT INTERVIEWS

We now move to the focal point of the interview day, the interview itself. The moment is finally here. You are in a room with the other candidates, and you may or may not know in which order you'll be seen. In any event, when it's your turn, someone will fetch you, open the door of the interview room and show you in.

From the moment the door opens and your usher pointedly stands aside to let the panel take a look at you in your glory, the game is on.

- Wait to be asked to sit down.
- If no one says anything, say, 'Shall I sit here?'
- Sit well – straight but not rigid. Head up, alert, eyes moving round the panel.
- Keep your hands under control. Lightly clasped is best.
- Panel members will doubtless be fiddling with papers and perhaps muttering. Keep calm.
- When the chair looks up and smiles, smile back.
- When the chair greets you, reply politely and look alert.

IT'S A CONVERSATION

A job interview is ideally a professional conversation, not an interrogation. Each formal question, agreed in advance by the panel, will be followed up by supplementary probing of your answer. The head and/or a head of department will probably take the lead on this follow-up, aiming to unpick your generalisations and expose your off-the-cuff comments. You need to keep some control of these parts of an interview: remember, you are free to use such conversational ploys as:

- I agree, but we shouldn't forget ...
- Could you just clarify that for me?
- Can I just add something ...
- As your colleague was saying a moment ago ...
- Yes, but I'd go even further and say ...

Remain sensitive to people's reactions – you want to see nods and smiles from most of the panel. Remember that some panel members, particularly heads and other senior teachers, may quite deliberately, by prior arrangement, show no reaction.

QUESTIONS

It's not easy to 'question spot' and even more difficult to foresee where the follow-up might lead. Some might be obvious: 'Why do you want to come to this school?' or 'What can you bring to this post?' Then there are the safeguarding questions we've already discussed.

Really, however, you have to be ready for anything. Perhaps the best advice is to do what good interviewees on TV current affairs programmes do, which is go in with a very clear idea of what they want to say, and then use the questions as vehicles for achieving that.

For example, you may want to deliver the following messages.

- You know quite a lot about the school, and the job – that's because you've done your homework, gathering information, starting before you applied and continuing right up to and into the interview day.

- You are clear about, and you can illustrate with real examples, how your particular skills, expertise, preferences and passions have worked for you and how you think they can apply to the job you're applying for.

- You can back up all the points you made in your written application. A panel member may well go through your letter: 'It says here that you ...' Be ready with chapter and verse of what you did and how you did it.

- You know why you want the job. It's because you know you can make a difference. And now you've been in the school and met the children you're even more sure of that. This is where overt bright-eyed enthusiasm is really important.

- You know why your subject is important, and why it's taught in schools.

- You don't know everything, but you are keen and ready to learn in a supportive staffroom and department. This works particularly well, of course, for newly qualified teachers.

- You like children and enjoy being with them. An astonishing number of job applicants never mention children. Where you can, illustrate your points with examples from your experience of satisfying or challenging encounters with particular children. Name them or, if you prefer, say, 'This boy – let's call him Jack ...' Smile as you remember.

- You are familiar with the term (and the concept of) 'safeguarding' children, and your understanding of it will show in your answers where appropriate.

- You know how you want children to react to you and speak of you to others.

- You can explain the techniques you use to promote and support good behaviour in your classes.

- You will always be totally professional. You will speak of former schools and colleagues only with politeness, giving credit where it's due. It can be appropriate to pay generous tribute to named people from whom you have learned. (Someone on the panel probably knows them, or knows of them, so don't be caught by a quick follow-up question.)

- You will be able to discuss your demonstration lesson objectively, with full knowledge of what worked, what didn't and what you would do differently next time.

- You will remember your presentation in detail (see page 143), and be ready to expand on any points you're asked about.

- You will firmly resist the temptation to make an impression by recounting an irrelevant school anecdote that you believe to be funny. It will go down like a lead balloon, unsettling you for the rest of the interview.

- You will not boast or appear too pleased with yourself. Be enthusiastic, but keep your answers factual and related to the job.

- Your body language will always be positive. This may need practice, with the help of close and critical friends and colleagues. Walk confidently, be relaxed but alert, make good eye contact, smile naturally when it's appropriate. Control the little habits that your close friends must be persuaded to tell you about (gulping, sniffing, blinking, sniggering nervously, clacking your false teeth, hitching up your underwear, snapping your braces, whatever).

- You will apologise for faux pas – momentarily forgetting the name of your previous school, or the one you're sitting in, or your own name, running out to be sick or go to the toilet (better than the alternatives) – and not let them put you off your stride. If you're doing well, the panel will not blame you for being human.

- Even if you feel you've had a bad interview, you will leave politely and gracefully, thanking the panel. Leave by the correct door. (I once left an interview into a broom cupboard. I did get the job, but the incident was so well remembered it was recounted at my leaving do.)

- You will not only switch off your phone, but you'll leave it outside the room. The internet is full of stories of interviews ruined by errant phones and bad phone behaviour.

LEGAL AND ILLEGAL QUESTIONS

Because questions are agreed in advance, they should all be legal – that's to say you will not, for example, be asked your age, religion, sexual orientation, marital status or whether you have children. Some candidates may themselves bring up such matters in discussion, but it's best to try not to.

Despite their training and preparation, inexperienced or maverick panel members will sometimes let an improper question slip out – a semi-conversational reference to family or 'your husband', for example. You may regard it as innocuous, but you shouldn't answer it because you really want to keep the interview professional. Deal with an inappropriate question by first remaining silent for a while, in the hope and expectation either that the questioner will realise and change tack (that's happened to me) or the chair will intervene tactfully by asking something entirely different. If that doesn't happen, deploy the *Newsnight* gambit, which is to smile and confidently say something that sounds sensible but doesn't actually answer the question.

WATCH FOR A 'RANDOM' QUESTION

Some chairs of interview panels make a point of asking one question that comes out of the blue, such as 'What's your favourite ice-cream flavour?' The obvious intention is to see to what extent the candidate is unsettled, and how well they respond. Clearly you can't prepare for the content of a random question, but you could make sure you're not unsettled, take a moment to think and then come back with a concise and at least coherent answer.

BE READY FOR THE 'SLEEPING VOLCANO' APPROACH

In many, perhaps most, interviews, the most influential person on the panel is the head teacher. And yet I've come across, and heard about, interviews in which the head has said very little. That's not as perverse as it seems. The head, after all, has closely studied your application, seen your teaching and your presentation and had a strong hand in preparing the interview questions and farming them out to other panel members. He or she has also had detailed discussions with the head of department, who is also on the panel. The head's idea now, in the interview, is to be free of the need to think up what to say, and so be able to sit closely watching, listening and weighing up each candidate, coming in perhaps with one really tricky question at the end.

Chair: 'I think that's all, ladies and gentlemen. If there are no more questions?'

The candidate makes to stand, smiling gratefully.

Head: 'Sorry, Chair, just before the candidate leaves, can I ask …'

It can be very unnerving for the candidate – which is part of the plan, of course.

Other questions you may be asked include, 'Do you have anything to ask us?' The chair will invariably ask this. It's not a trick question, but a genuine invitation. It's OK to say, 'No thank you, I had a good tour of the school and I think I'm clear about the job now.'

You may also be asked, 'Are you a genuine candidate? If offered the job today, would you accept?' This is sometimes asked either at the beginning or the end. It's a quasi-legal question and makes sure that the exercise isn't a waste of time on either side.

SHUT UP

Perhaps most importantly of all, there really is such a thing as talking yourself out of a job. Many, perhaps all, teachers are programmed to talk a lot. Make yourself say what you want to say, then shut up. Be very alert to the attitude of the panel, whether any are starting to fiddle with papers, for example. If you stop, the panel can ask you follow-ups, and there may be times when you say, 'I can give you another example of that if you like?' They're then free to say, 'No, that's fine,' or, 'Please, do go on.'

You may need to rehearse giving concise but good answers to specific questions. Do it with hard-hearted friends armed with bells and whistles to use when you're waffling.

KEY POINTS

■ Use a range of faces – smile, look serious, make eye contact.

■ Look at each member of the panel, not just at one person.

■ It's fine to pause and think before you answer.

■ Beware of 'anchor' phrases: 'When I was at St Jude's' grates after the third or fourth time of hearing.

GOOD TEACHERS TEACH A GOOD - OR BETTER - DEMONSTRATION LESSON

GOOD TEACHERS TEACH A GOOD – OR BETTER – DEMONSTRATION LESSON

Above all, interviewers want to know how good a teacher you are, so even if a senior person at the school has visited and seen you teach on your home ground, you are likely to be asked to teach a demonstration lesson to a class in the school. *It's a vital, often decisive, part of the interview.* Here's what one head teacher said about why she wanted to see a lesson:

For teaching posts (and senior posts to be honest), the key is the quality of the person's teaching. Being a really good teacher and (for more senior roles) understanding how to develop people into good teachers is vitally important.

The lesson to be taught at interview may sometimes only last for 30 minutes – I'd stress being prepared for the length of lesson they tell you and being prepared to change tack if you find the students are either 'getting it' quickly, or just don't 'get it'. This is so tricky when you don't know the children or the school, but being able to be flexible and to *respond* to the students' learning is very important.

IT'S ABOUT HOW YOU COPE

Everyone knows that the demonstration lesson places you in a difficult and untypical position. What matters is how well you are prepared and how flexible and agile you are at dealing with the unexpected.

PREPARING YOUR LESSON

As with all lessons, and also with every aspect of your job application, preparation is the key. To begin with, try to find out answers to the following – some you will certainly be given, others you might have to ask about, but they're all valid questions.

- What you'll have to teach.
- The length of the session.
- How it fits into the normal scheme of work – what came before.
- Nature of the group – number, age, ability.
- Children with special needs (including gifted and talented).
- The discipline and reward policy as you're able to apply it.

- Available resources.
- Expectations about the use of ICT.
- Other adults you're expected to involve
  – teaching assistant (TA), special educational
  needs (SEN) coordinator, assistant technician.

Then you can prepare a lesson that you can deliver in a way that's familiar and comfortable. It ought to be clear to you, from all your research, and your visit to the school, what styles of pedagogy will be accepted. If you want to take risks with a more unusual lesson, that may work in your favour, but rehearse it with a class in your own school, and have a good plan B ready.

NAMES ARE VERY IMPORTANT

Try to establish a seating plan, with names, before you start. If you can arrange it so you walk in and tape it to the desk in front of you, or have it on your tablet, you've won a small victory. Being able to use names right away is empowering and impressive both to the children and to observers.

RESOURCES

Take nothing for granted. Take your own stuff – paper, pencils, whatever the children are likely to ask for. Prepare good, professional-looking support resources on big sheets of paper – showing key words, pictures, graphs. Either use them from the start, or keep them in reserve if the ICT doesn't work.

Prepare tasks that will include the range of abilities.

If your lesson will be in a science lab or design and technology (D&T) room, make friends with the technician – he/she can make all the difference for you.

ICT

Many schools are very focused on ICT. There's likely to be a digital whiteboard, or a projector. The class you're going into may be equipped one-to-one with tablets. Whether they are or not, remember the mantra – which you may well want to use in your interview or in the follow-up to your lesson: 'It's not about technology and devices; it's about teaching and learning and whether the technology can help with that.'

Of course, you may feel you have to use technology to demonstrate your familiarity with it. But make sure it's a natural choice for what you've planned, will enhance learning, and isn't just done for show.

In any case, be prepared for ICT meltdown. Nothing's worse than seeing a teacher fiddling with the technology, making apologetic noises while the class twiddle their thumbs, or become restless. Best give up quickly and move smoothly to plan B which is technology-free. The rule is, 'Prepare as for a power cut.'

THE SHAPE OF THE LESSON

Your demonstration lesson must have structure. In particular, it needs a clear beginning and end, and it must show:

■ Good questioning.

■ Good classroom management.

■ Enthusiasm for the subject.

■ Respect for, and kindness to, the children.

■ Confident spotting and checking of incipient behaviour problems.

■ Praise when warranted – but for specific tasks and responses, not 'scattergun'.

■ A task, however short, for the children to do.

■ Awareness of pace, and of the time available.

Make sure the lesson comes to an organised close. It's easy to run out of time. Other candidates will, believe me, so make sure you are the one who's seen to come to a smart, smiling, encouraging close right on the dot.

TWO FINAL TOUCHES

1 Thank the children. They know what's going on. If they've done well, tell them so.

2 If you've set work, collect it in for marking, and make sure you do.

WHAT TO DO IF THE LESSON GOES PEAR-SHAPED

It's possible that the lesson will go wrong, and you 'lose' the children. Whatever you do, *don't panic*. Don't give up in embarrassment, handing over to the observer.

All your observers are interested in is how you deal with the problem. You should stop everything. Settle the children down. Be assertive and calm. Don't rush. Take a brief moment, then move straight to a manageable task. One of my favourites has always been, 'Write down ten words' about the topic in hand. Say it as if it's something you had always planned to do next. Then move the lesson on to discuss the words: 'That's a great word, Jason, because it ...'

If you pull things back and move to even a modestly adequate conclusion, then you will win credit.

POST-MORTEM

You'll be asked, perhaps in the interview, perhaps immediately after the lesson, how the lesson went. You should:

- **Be honest**. If they think you can't recognise your mistakes, you won't get the job. But:
- **Be precise**. Categorise parts of the lesson as good, satisfactory or unsatisfactory, with a clear account of what lies behind your judgement.
- **Remember** that what matters is whether the children learned what you set out to teach them.

Most importantly, show clearly, with specific examples, that you know how you could have done better.

KEY POINTS

- When you go in, your attitude should be, 'I am the teacher and I'm going to teach you.'

- Be decisive with instructions at the start: 'This is how I want it.'

- Praise individuals who quickly pick up on what you're asking.

- Keep alert; distribute your attention round the room; pick up on disengagement.

- In fact, just be a good teacher.

GOOD TEACHERS GIVE GOOD PRESENTATIONS (AND DO EFFECTIVE IN-TRAY EXERCISES)

GOOD TEACHERS GIVE GOOD PRESENTATIONS (AND DO EFFECTIVE IN-TRAY EXERCISES)

Many schools require applicants to make a presentation to the interview panel. Here's what the head of a highly successful school, which attracts many applicants for all its vacancies, had to say:

We always ask candidates to give either a five- or ten-minute presentation to the interview panel. The way a candidate has prepared can tell you *so* much. The single most irritating thing with the presentation is when a candidate goes on too long and they've tried to cram far too much information into the PowerPoint slides.

IT'S ALL IN THE PREPARATION

Really, what that head says tells you everything you need to know. The most important point is that she's interested at least as much in preparation and delivery as in the content.

What that means for you is that you need to be concise, confident and very well prepared. Do the job properly and it is an opportunity to:

- Show good subject knowledge.
- Explain your teaching principles.
- Show that you are aware of the challenges in the advertised job.
- Give a very early idea of how your experience will help with the challenges.
- Demonstrate your ability to give clear and concise explanations.

As with everything in your application, always bear in mind the job you are applying for, because the interviewing panel will make that connection continuously as you speak.

THE BASICS

Make sure you know where you will give your presentation. It's not essential to use technology, so only use it if it genuinely enhances your message. If you do want to use it, make sure you know what's available. If in doubt, take your own kit, but you'll still need to ensure that it will work in that setting, and whether you will have time to set up and check everything. It's difficult to imagine any school being difficult about helping you with this. It's not in their interest to set traps for you.

Using that head's brief words of advice, it becomes possible to distil some rules for your presentation:

- If you're given a topic, don't be afraid to focus on one key aspect of it. Time will be short. But explain why you've chosen that aspect.

- If you're not given a topic, be guided by the job description – find an area that you'll be responsible for and, again, focus your presentation down to a well-defined aspect.

- You're a teacher, so think of it as a story. You're a good storyteller, which is fortunate because, although your listeners might not like presentations much, everyone likes stories.

- Stick to the time limit. Given your desire to make the most of yourself, that's going to be difficult. Be ruthless. Select the key points and determinedly resist the desire to add extra stuff.

- Avoid any sense of rush. American educator Lisa Nielsen says:

Presenters fail when they say things like:

'We have a lot to get through today.'

'I am speaking quickly so we have time to cover everything.'

'We're already behind schedule.'

'In the interest of time …'[1]

- Speak clearly, with expression, facing the audience and making eye contact, not turning to a screen or flip chart. Reading from a screen, standing side-on to the audience, head averted, is irritating, and yet you see it all the time.

- PowerPoint (or equivalent presentation software) is far from compulsory. In any case, prepare and rehearse a non-technological plan B, because the technology may fail through no fault of yours.

- Use plain language. Expert listeners are bored by jargon; non-experts are annoyed by it.

- Give the presentation an identifiable structure – beginning, middle, end is an obvious one.

- Leave time to sum up with an arresting conclusion.

- Stand still most of the time.

---

1   Lisa Nielsen. 'One mistake presenters should never make and 8 strategies to avoid it', *The Innovative Educator* (December 2015). Available at: http:// theinnovativeeducator.blogspot.co.uk/2015/12/1-thing-presenters-should-always-do-8.html.

- Mention children, and smile when you do.

- Although you're well-rehearsed, you must be yourself – unstilted, relaxed, smiling, confident. If necessary, call on your thespian skills.

- Aim to end right on the dot, with a final snappy sentence, a smile and a thank you.

- Rehearse, over and over again, in as realistic a setting as possible – in your own school hall, for example, when everyone's left, with highly critical and more experienced people watching and ready to feed back.

TECHNOLOGY

This needs a special mention. Just to repeat – presentation software such as PowerPoint is not compulsory, but it can help. Use it sparingly though and keep it in proportion. Limit the number of slides to an essential minimum, and keep tight control over the amount of information that's on each one. The slide must enhance your message – a single image and/or a quotation inserted at each key point may well be enough.

Consider the *Pecha Kucha* (Japanese for chit-chat) 20 × 20 style of presentation – twenty slides, shown for twenty seconds each. Some make it 20 × 20 × 30 – each slide to have no more than thirty words. Others would say thirty words is too many, and others would go for far fewer than twenty slides, each with a single bold image and very few words.

WHAT COUNTS AS A GOOD PRESENTATION?

The interviewing panel, when they discuss your presentation, will ideally say some of the following things.

'I found myself smiling back, because she was making eye contact and being so pleasant.'

'She was the only one who kept to the time limit.'

'I admired the way she resisted the temptation to turn round and look at her slides all the time.'

'I loved the slides. Just a single image and a key sentence. All the meat was in what she told us. The slides just kept us concentrating.'

'I always knew where she was in the presentation, and so did she. It was so well constructed. It led to a short and telling conclusion.'

'I could just see her giving a presentation to a staff meeting or the governors. It would go down well.'

'That last sentence was a killer. I had to stop myself applauding.'

'Did I agree with everything she said? Of course not. But that's not what it was all about, was it?'

THE IN-TRAY EXERCISE

This is usually reserved for applicants who are being interviewed for senior leadership posts – head, deputy and assistant heads; anyone, in fact, who might be in charge of the school, perhaps unexpectedly and temporarily. It's by no means a decisive part of the selection process, but it does show another aspect of the candidate's abilities.

The applicant is faced with a number of decisions, all to be taken within a defined short time. The aim is to see whether he or she can make safe and sensible decisions quickly and methodically without fussing, constant changes of mind or long-drawn-out dithering.

It's difficult to foresee what any in-tray (real or virtual) might contain, but the tasks usually come under some or all of these headings:

- ▪ A note from an angry parent who demands to be seen.

- A phone message about a member of staff whose partner has been involved in a road accident.
- A letter from the local community leaders about student misbehaviour on the way home.
- A demand from the government for specific data.

There could be many more.

On the whole, decisive action is what's required, and there's no single right way. However, there are basic principles that are too serious to miss – the fact that threats to the physical safety of children override everything else; the willingness to delegate; not allowing anger and shouting to become effective arguments. All of this, and more, should be manageable by an experienced teacher, so the rule is to keep calm, see things through the perspective of your own experience, and have confidence in your judgement as a teacher.

KEY POINTS

- It's more about you, less about the content.
- Use technology sparingly as a highlighter.
- Make eye contact.
- Stay in touch with the job description.

GOOD TEACHERS KNOW HOW TO HANDLE THE POST-INTERVIEW PROCESS

GOOD TEACHERS KNOW HOW TO HANDLE THE POST-INTERVIEW PROCESS

When your interview finishes, two things may happen. Traditionally, you were taken back to the waiting room to re-join the other candidates, to wait as the panel makes its decision. Now, it's much more common for all candidates to be asked to go home and wait to be told the decision by phone.

IF YOU ARE OFFERED THE JOB

Either way, the successful candidate will not simply be given the job but will be offered it. This is the decisive moment. Say yes – and shake hands if you're present – and the job is yours. The die is cast. There'll be a contract and paperwork, but that might come further down the line. The offer and acceptance are what count.

Here's a true story. A candidate, offered the job, was very much attracted by it, but had doubts about one or two aspects, so she asked for a couple of days to think it over. The panel sent her away briefly to consider her request.

What possible responses could they have made? The panel might have pressed her about her doubts, in the hope of clearing them up. They might have simply agreed to her request. They might have insisted on a decision there and then.

In actual fact, on the day, this panel went for a fourth option, which was to withdraw the offer, saying something like: 'No, you can't have time to think, and as we speak we're offering the job to another candidate. So, regretfully, it's goodbye.'

You see the point? The candidate's indecision was taken as a lack of true commitment to the job. Why appoint someone like that when there are other good and eager candidates?

The moral? Be decisive. Either take the job or don't. There's no shame in withdrawing at any point right up to the moment of the job offer, so long as you are clear and definite about it.

Here's another true story. Interviewed candidates were sitting together waiting for the panel's decision. One began musing aloud about things he didn't like about the job, the area the school was in, all kinds of general doubts. Eventually another candidate could bear it no longer, and burst out: 'For crying out loud, if you don't want the job, knock on the door and tell them you're withdrawing.' Which is exactly what he did.

In many ways, surprisingly perhaps, you can compare this process to a wedding: if you are railroaded by it, carried along against your better judgement, it's surely not a recipe for future success. Better say no at the altar than get into a whole package of trouble later on.

PLAY FAIR

Suppose – and this is surprisingly common when you're applying for lots of jobs – you have two interviews within a couple of days of each other. You actually would prefer the second job, but attend the first one and are offered the job. What do you do?

There are only two ethical options. You take the first job, and immediately phone the second school to explain and withdraw. Or you turn the first job down and cross your fingers for the second one.

The unethical option is to go to the second interview, and if you get the job, contact the school where you've already shaken hands on the job and say that you've had second thoughts and would like to change your mind.

A head says: 'If I discovered that someone on my staff had got their job with me on that basis, my opinion of them would dive, and it would take a very long time to recover.'

Reading between the lines:

■ The chances of discovery are high.

■ For 'a very long time', read 'never'.

HAVING SECOND THOUGHTS

While we're on the subject, let's consider the more straightforward case where, with no playing off of one job against another, a candidate genuinely does have second thoughts.

What's usually happened here is that the candidate has been carried along to the point of the handshake, all the while convincing herself that it's the right decision, and quashing any negative thoughts. (The wedding comparison continues to be striking, does it not?) Then, once at home, in familiar surroundings, and back at school, also in familiar surroundings, the doubts can build into a tidal wave.

Maybe the job's not what you thought. Perhaps the house prices are too high, or your partner is voicing previously hidden worries. All in all, over a short period – typically a weekend – you become certain that you've made a mistake. Should you – can you – phone up and say you've changed your mind?

Strictly speaking, no. You committed yourself when you accepted the offer. After all, as your less sympathetic colleagues and friends will rightly say, you should have cleared up all the potential snags in advance: doing the research, being up front with doubts and questions. Any real uncertainty should have made you withdraw before the end of the day.

However, if you do make that call and withdraw, you'll get away with it. The school won't want to waste time discussing the position with you. You've left them with a problem, after all, and they'll want to get on with finding someone else.

All the same, you'll leave a bad impression that won't help if you try for other jobs in the same neck of the woods. Heads do talk to each other, so please don't do it unless you're sure it's not a bit of panic about uprooting. In any case, try not to do it again, because it could be fatal for your chances if word gets around.

SALARY NEGOTIATIONS

Increasingly, teacher salaries are, within limits, set by the school. But can you negotiate, and how would you do it? Asked about this, one experienced academy principal suggests trying to pin down the salary before applying. But if there's to be any negotiation, the time is between being offered the job and accepting it, using a form of words such as, 'I am very keen to accept the position but would like to ask, is there any flexibility with the starting salary?'

This principal also reminds new teachers of a useful ploy: 'For NQTs it's getting more commonplace to ask to be paid from the start of July – so that they can spend a few weeks in the school before the summer, and get paid for the summer holiday.'

WHAT IF YOU DON'T GET THE JOB?

That's close to being one of those daft questions that TV reporters ask: 'How do you feel, Mrs Smith, now that your house has burned down and you've lost everything?'

However, in teaching, if someone says, 'Don't despair, it's not the end of the world,' they're not just using idle words. If you did well at interview, you could have built up some professional brownie points.

The first thing to do is ask for a debrief. One head noted, on this point:

I always respect candidates who request feedback in a written form rather than just over the phone. It is time-consuming but I feel that if candidates have gone to the effort of applying and going through a gruelling day's interview, the least they can expect is advice and help about how to be successful next time.

If you behave gracefully and professionally after your unsuccessful interview – making a point of thanking people at the school, making positive comments about people you've met – then you leave a good impression behind. Always remember that heads talk to each other, and that other jobs might come up at the same school or in the same group of schools. There have been many occasions when someone has said, 'It was probably for the best in the end, because I went on to get that post at ...'

Remember Julie Andrews? She was turned down for a role in the film of *My Fair Lady* and so was free to do *The Sound of Music*. Her bank manager must have been among many people who were delighted at the outcome.

KEY POINTS

- If the job's not for you, then withdraw.
- Straight after accepting the job, volunteer to visit for further discussion.
- Be pleasant and polite in defeat and ask for feedback, written if possible.
- Remember, heads are influential people. If you made a good impression, it could turn out well in the end.

RECOMMENDATIONS

Access to the internet is essential. Although some journals have jobs pages, in each case the really rich, fully searchable source is always online. Advertising can be expensive so although many appear on more than one website or journal, you cannot assume this, and so you need to study as many as possible. Use a search engine for 'teaching jobs'. Be prepared to spend time, and keep the results well organised. Here are just some examples:

https://www.tes.co.uk/jobs/

The biggest – and for many years, effectively the only – source of advertised teaching jobs both in hard copy with the magazine and online is the *TES* (formerly the *Times Educational Supplement*). It's more than just a list of jobs – although it's a very comprehensive one. There's job-hunting advice and also the facility to manage your job-hunting, and sign up for email alerts of interesting jobs. *TES* also has a free jobs app.

http://jobs.theguardian.com/jobs/ schools/#browsing

The Guardian also lists several thousand teaching jobs, searchable under a wide range of headings.

**http://www.education.gov.uk/get-into-teaching/
about-teaching/looking-for-a-job**

This government website is of most use to new teachers
seeking their first job.

Among other job advertisement sites are:

http://www.education-jobs.co.uk/

http://www.eteach.com/

**http://www.teachfirst.org.uk/careers/
our-current-vacancies**

http://www.timeplan.com

**http://www.britishcouncil.org/jobs/careers/
english/teachers**

https://targetjobs.co.uk/

Also, local government websites always have a listing of
jobs available.

Specialist recruiters also often have sections on education
– Hays, for example, list many jobs for primary, secondary
and supply teachers.

http://hays.co.uk/job/education-jobs/index.htm

http://www.reed.co.uk

ACKNOWLEDGEMENTS

Among very many teachers, school leaders, parents, governors and students who have contributed to my understanding of the recruitment process, I pay particular tribute to three highly successful school leaders. All three read drafts at various stages and, in each case, added valuable thoughts and words.

Kenny Frederick, an executive member of the National Association of Head Teachers (NAHT), was, when I approached her, Principal of George Green's School in the Isle of Dogs, Tower Hamlets, London.

Isobel Bryce is head teacher of Saltash.net Community School in Cornwall.

Dr Terry Fish is head teacher of Twynham School in Christchurch, Dorset.